MICROSCOPY OF REMEDIES

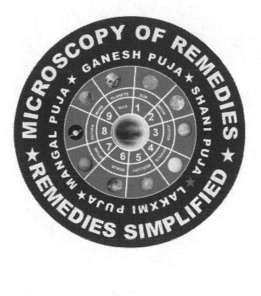

MICROSCOPY OF REMEDIES
REMEDIES OF ALL PLANETS AND NUMBERS
REMEDIES SIMPLIFIED

BALDEV BHATIA
(Consultant Astrology-Numerology)
A Partridge India
A PENGUIN RANDOM HOUSE COMPANY
(Paper Pack)

PARTRIDGE
A Penguin Random House Company

To order additional copies of this book, contact
Partridge India
000 800 10062 62
orders.india@partridgepublishing.com

www.partridgepublishing.com/india

CONTENTS

BLESSING OF GOD GANESHA

BLESSING OF GOD SHIVA

BLESSING OF OMKAR

INTRODUCTION

Mostly all problems in life are caused by afflicted, the weak, badly placed planets. The astrology consultant, astrologer, numerologist gives his advice to all people to come out of their problems with astrological remedies to ward off the evil effects, afflictions of the planets and to strengthen the functional benefic planets in order, so that these good planets do function well and they wipe out the negative forces.

Based on the ancient studies of hundreds and hundreds of natal charts, these astrological remedies have been successfully made to come in force for reducing and warding off the malefic effects and influences of the negative planets in a way to get good and positive results in life. If used as a preservation and preventive measure, these remedies have the caliber to save the person from mis happenings critical issues pertaining from health issues to financial crises.

This combination of application of astral remedies (to strengthen the benefices and reduce the afflictions of the malefic) is provided after studying the problematic planetary influences in a chart.

The puja for Peaceful blessing of the planets or The Graha Shanti as it is often known in Indian language is required if a planet is, stationed in the house of the enemy or looking at the enemy which gives the power to raise the power of the evil effect of the planet resulting in misfortune to the native.

There are a number of effective astrological remedies which are good for everyone. If we follow all of these no other remedy is required, anyone can try and see for himself the positive changes in his life within a few weeks.

The following remedies are necessary if the chart signifies any of the following conditions given below:

1. When the Planet is debilitated
2. When the Planet is in a 'negative' sign

3. When there is a weak ascendant lord but in a friend/own/neutral sign.
4. When the Planets are in the 8th (longevity, dead sign)
5. When the planets are in relatives sign the third angle or when they are in accidents, future events etc.) but with a friend/own/neutral sign.
6. There are many points to remember and few are illustrated below:

First of all extreme care must be taken when you are appeasing a Goddess, if you are not able to do or comfortable you can ask your mother to do it for you. Common remedies which we ought to know:

1. For planet Saturn: Do not say anything bad about Saturn such as do not think badly of elderly or old people, homeless, disabled etc. Do not insult beggars and lower class people.
2. For Planet Venus: do not insult butcher class, non-vegetarians, actors, artists, fashion models, nudists, prostitutes, lovers, other religions, rich and successful people.
3. For planets Jupiter and Mercury: do not insult Teachers, Spiritual gurus, vegetarians, Children, Teenagers, Jewelers, salesmen, treasurers, Accountants, cashiers, auditors, tax officials and other guardians of money.
4. For planet Sun: Do not Insult/contradict rulers, land/property owners, priests, church fathers, saints, God etc. and avoid being greedy and filthy. Wash your hands after you touch any footwear and also before lunch etc.
5. For planet Moon: Do not argue with the family, don't be jealous of other families. Do not insult women, mental retards and traumatized people. Do not reject water to the thirsty and always drink pure water.
6. For planet Rahu and Ketu: Do not abuse animals, do not torture your body—avoid excessive fasting, smoking and drinking.
7. For planet Mars: Do not insult soldiers [even enemy soldiers], doctors, surgeons, sportsmen, laborers or other worker class.

PREFACE

As we know that people in this world are depressed disheartened and anguished mentally; many are physically disturbed, some by children and some by spouse.

There is no harmony between in the family The tradition of the joint family has been badly shattered. Everybody needs peace and solutions to their problems; they need a solution and freedom from these problems.

Taking the above factors into consideration the author has discussed some of the powerful remedies based on the principles of the famous book known as "Lal Kitab".

The Lal Kitab Remedies are simple, easy and cheap. Lal Kitab Remedies are very effective and have no side-effects.

Remedies are as follows:

Sweet loaves of bread, specially baked in Tandoor, should be offered to animals every month for warding off sickness, quarrels and other troubles, caused by Mars negative in the horoscope.

Throwing copper coins in running water, taking blessings of elders by touching their feet, praying and worshiping god and goddesses, refrain from alcohols, offering food to disabled, helping widows, offering food to crows, cows or dogs.

Some remedies that help a person from troubles and tensions are remedies like distributing sweets or throwing patashas and coal in running water.

Other Lal Kitab remedies are as follows:

These steps will reduce the bad effect of dragon head who is natural malefic and whose job is to cause unnecessary and avoidable worries and fears.

1. Put your dining table as close to the kitchen as possible and avoid eating while seated on your bed.
2. Dispose of articles which have not been used for decades, do not clutter your house /office with unnecessary articles.
3. Do not look down upon monks or elderly people.
4. Try to get the blessings of elderly people in your neighborhood, office or workplace.
5. Do not ever annoy your father.

Other common remedies are

1. Do not kick dogs, nor throw stones at them, if possible feed and do take care of them.
2. Feed Cows—for better conjugal relations and health of wife.
3. Feed Crows/fish, for mothers better health /financial prospects.
4. Feed monkeys to improve financial condition and for getting favors from the government.
5. Wear gold ring, golden strap on your wrist or apply saffron on your forehead.

Places where ornaments or money is kept secretly must not be left empty. If there is nothing to be kept, please put some dry fruits there.

Worship of lord Ganesh is highly auspicious for children and property. If one's children do not survive the native must distribute salty preparations in place of sweets, to celebrate the birth of the child.

There are several more remedies that are often used to ward off the evil effects of the unfavorable planets.

The most commonly used have been described in detail in the chapters.

Remedies of the different Planets, and Numbers through Mantras Tantras and Yantras. The author has also tried to pen down his life experience though this Manu scripture and hopes that the application of all the remedies would be a great asset to the source of mankind and he wishes his readers all the success in their lives.

In the end I would definitely like to express my sincere thanks to MS. ALPA SHAH Director Travel Company of UK, Mr. Rajinder Kulkarni and Mira Kulkarni, Directors, for encouraging me to pen down this book in the interest of the readers.

I am also grateful and thankful to A Partridge India A PENGUIN RANDOM HOUSE COMPANY for publishing a very useful book in the service of mankind.

DATED   SD/-

MAY 27th 2014   BALDEV BHATIA

Chapter One

SUN

Effects and Remedies

The Sun, eulogized by the author of the Lal Kitab as Vishnu, the lord of presentation, is the father of our solar system, around which all planets resolve. The power of light in the sky, the temperature of the earth, the power of presentation and progress are represented by the sun. His presence means the "day" and absence means the "night". The soul in human body and the power of rendering bodily services to others have also been referred to the Sun—a royal planet of power, authority and finances.

The Sun provides good results if placed in houses 1 to 5, 8, 9, 11 and 12. The 6th, 7th, and 10th are bad houses for the Sun. The Moon, the Jupiter and the Mars are the planets friendly to the Sun, where the Saturn, Venus, Rahu and Ketu are enemies. The first is the SOLID HOUSE, the permanent house and the house of exaltation of the Sun, whereas the 7th house is in the house of debilitation. The Mars in the 6th and Ketu in the 1st house make the Sun produce results of an exalted planet. If the Sun is exalted or placed in an auspicious house of a person's horoscope he is bound to rise higher and higher in power and position. If obstacles are created against him by a person that person is bound to meet his doom. Much better results are proposed if the Sun is in conjunction with Mercury.

The Sun gives adverse effects on the things associated with the house in which he is placed. Consequently in the 1st house he will create health problems for the native. In the 2nd house he will affect the family and its comforts absolutely adversely.

The sun in the 6th house will not prove good for the sisters and daughters of the native. In the 7th he will face obstacles in the comforts of the wife. The Sun of the 8th house will save the native from death in critical situations.

The sun of the 9th house will destroy the comforts of the forefathers and perhaps deprive the native of their properties. In the 10th, the sun will affect the father adversely. The sun in the 11th increases and multiplies the income of the native manifold, if he does not augment the power of Saturn by consumption of liquor, meat and eggs. The Sun in the 12th house destroys the comforts of the night hour sleep of the native.

The Sun will not be able to harm Venus when sun is being expected by Saturn because Saturn and Venus are great friends. On the contrary, if Saturn is being expected by Sun, then the Sun will not be afraid of Saturn and he will destroy the Venus as both are natural enemies in the house where he is placed.

GENERAL REMEDIES FOR THE PLANET SUN IN BRIEF

1. Prepare a sweet dish made out of wheat
2. Place the dish on a lotus leaf.
3. Stand in the river/river bank if you don't live near a river, you can choose other places like sun temple, quiet place etc.
4. Make sure it's Sunday morning.
5. Turn east and hold the leaf with the dish near your chest and recite Surya mantra/sloka three times.
6. Give some to others before you swallow.

SPECIAL REMEDIES FOR PLANET SUN IN DETAIL

The effects of the Sun in both the situations in different houses are as below:

Sun in 1st House

Benefic:

(1) The native will be fond of constructing, Religious buildings and digging of wells for public purposes. He will have permanent source

of livelihood—more from the government. Money earned from honest sources will keep multiplying. He will believe only his eyes, not in ears.

Malefic:

The native's father may die in early childhood. Having sex in the day time will make the wife constantly ill and have infection of tuberculosis if Venus is placed in the 7th house. Malefic sun in the 1st house and Mars in the 5th house will cause the death of sons, one after the other. Similarly, the malefic Sun in the 1st house and Saturn in the 8th house will cause the death of wives, one after the other. If there is no planet in the 7th house the marriage before 24th year will prove lucky for the native, otherwise the 24th year of the native would prove highly disastrous for him

Remedial Measures:

(1) Marry before 24th year of life.
(2) Don't have sex with wife during the day time.
(3) Install a hand pump for water in your ancestral house.
(4) Construct small dark room in the left side at the end of your house.
(5) Either of the spouses must stop eating "GUR" i.e. jiggery.

Sun in 2nd house

Benefic :

1. The native will be self-dependent, skilled in handiwork and would prove highly helpful to parents, maternal uncles, sisters, daughters and in-laws.
2. The Sun in the 2nd will become more auspicious if the Moon is placed in the 6th house.
3. Ketu in the 8th house will make the native very truthful.

Rahu in the 9th house makes the native a renowned artist or painter.

1. Ketu in the 9th house makes him a great technician.
2. Mars in the 9th house makes him fashionable.

3. The generous nature of the native would put an end to growing enemies.

Malefic:

(1) The Sun will affect very adversely the things and relatives associated with the planets inimical to the Sun i.e., wife, wealth, widows, cows, taste, mother etc. Disputes regarding wealth property and wife will spoil the native.

(2) Never accept donations if the Moon is placed in the 8th house and the Sun in the 2nd house are not auspicious; otherwise the native will be destroyed altogether.

(3) The Sun in the 2nd house, Mars in the 1st and Moon in the 12th house make the native's condition critical and pathetic in every manner.

(4) Mars in the 8th house makes the native extremely greedy if the Sun in the 2nd house is inauspicious.

Remedial Measures:

(1) Donate coconut, mustard oil and almonds to religious places of 0wnorship.

(2) Manage to avoid disputes involving wealth, property and ladies.

(3) Avoid accepting donations, specially rice, silver and milk.

Sun in 3rd House

Benefic:

(1) The native will be rich, self-dependent and having younger brothers.

(2) He will be blessed with divine grace and will earn profits intellectual by pursuits.

(3) He will be interested in astrology and mathematics.

Malefic:

(1) If the Sun is not auspicious in the 3rd house and the Moon is also not auspicious in the horoscope, there will be daylight robbery or theft in the native's house.

(2) If the 9th house is afflicted, the forefathers would have been poor. If the 1st house is afflicted, the neighbors of the native will be destroyed.

Remedial Measures:

(1) Obtain blessings of the mother by keeping her happy.

(2) Serve others with rice or milk.

(3) Practice good conduct and avoid evil deeds.

Sun in 4th House

Benefic:

(1) The native will be wise, kind and a good administrator. He will have constant source of income. He will leave a legacy of great riches for his off springs after death.

(2) If the Moon is with the Sun in the 4th house, the native will earn great profit through certain new researches.

(3) The Mercury in the 10th or 4th house will make such a native a renowned trader.

(4) If Jupiter is also with the Sun in the 4th house, the native will make good profits through gold and silver trade.

Malefic:

(1) The native becomes greedy, inclined to commit theft and likes to harm others. This tendency ultimately produces very bad results.

(2) If the Saturn is placed in the 7th house he becomes victimized by night blindness.

(3) If the Sun is inauspicious in the 7th house and mars are placed in the 10th house, the native's eye will become seriously defective, but his fortunes will not dwindle.

(4) The native will become impotent if the Sun in the 4th is inauspicious and the Moon is placed in the 1st or 2nd house, the Venus is in the 5th and Saturn is in the 7th house.

Remedial Measures:

(1) Distribute alms and food to the needy people.
(2) Do not take up business associated with iron and wood.
(3) Business associated with gold, silver, cloth will give very good results.

Sun in 5th house

Benefic:

(1) The progress and prosperity of family and children will be assured. If the Mars is placed in the 1st or 8th house and Rahu, Ketu, Saturn are placed in 9th and 12th houses, the native will lead king's life.
(2) If in 5th house placed with any planet inimical to sun, the native will be bestowed hour by the government everywhere.
(3) If Jupiter is placed in 9th or 12th house, the enemies will be destroyed, but this position will not be good for children of the native.

Malefic:

(1) If the Sun in the 5th is inauspicious and Jupiter is in 10th, the wife of the native will die and wives in subsequent marriages will also die
(2) If the sun in the 5th house is inauspicious and Saturn is placed in 3rd, sons of the native will die.

Remedial Measures:

(1) Do not delay in having a child.
(2) Build your kitchen in the eastern portion of your house.
(3) Drop a lit the quantity of mustard oil on the ground continuously for 43 days.

Sun in 6th House

Benefic:

(1) Native will be lucky, prone to anger, will have beautiful spouse and will benefit from that government.
(2) If Sun is in the 6th house and Moon, Mars and Jupiter in the 2nd house, following tradition will be beneficial.
(3) If sun is in 6th house and Ketu in 1st or 7th house then the native will have a son and after the 48th year great fortune will follow.

Malefic:

(1) The native's son and maternal family will face bad times. Will also affect native health adversely.
(2) If there is a no planet in the 2nd house, the native will get a government job in the 22nd year of his life.
(3) If Mars is placed in the 10th house the native's sons will die one after the other.
(4) Mercury in the 12th house causes high blood pressure.

Remedial Measures:

(1) Ancestral customs also should be strictly followed; otherwise the family progress and happiness will be destroyed.
(2) Underground furnaces should not be constructed with in the premises of the house.
(3) After taking dinner blow off the fire of the kitchen stove by sprinkling milk over it.
(4) Always keep Gangajal in the premises of your house.
(5) Offer wheat or Gur to monkeys.

Sun in 7th House

Benefic:

(1) If Jupiter, Mars or Moon are placed in the 2nd house, the native will occupy a ministerial position in the government.
(2) If the Mercury is exalted or Mercury in the 5th or 7th house is expected by Mars, the native will have unending sources of income.

Malefic:

(1) If the Sun is inauspicious in the 7th house and Jupiter, Venus or any malefic planet is placed in the 11th house and Mercury is malefic in any other house, the native will encounter the death of several members of his family together. Obstacles from the government diseases like tuberculosis and asthma will victimize the native. Incidents of fire, embalmment and other family troubles will madden the native who may go to the extent of becoming a recluse or committing suicide.
(2) Malefic Sun in the 7th and Mars or Saturn in the 2nd or 12th house and Moon in the 1st house cause leprosy or leucoderma.

Remedial Measures:

(1) Lessen the amount of salt intake.
(2) Start any work after taking a little sweet with water.
(3) Offer a little piece of your chapati to the fire of the kitchen before taking your meals.
(4) Serving and rearing up a black cow or a cow without horns but make sure that the cow is not white.

Sun in 8th House

Benefic:

(1) Government favors will accrue from the 22nd year of life.
(2) Here the Sun makes the native truthful, saintly and king like. Nobody would be able to harm him.

Malefic:

(1) Mercury in the 2nd house will create economic crisis.
(2) Native will be short tempered, impatient & will have ill health.

Remedial Measures:

(1) Never keep a white cloth in the house.
(2) Never live in the house facing south.
(3) Always eat something sweet and drink water before starting any new work.
(4) Throw copper coins in a burning pyre (Chita) whenever possible.
(5) Throw Gur (jaggery) in running water.

Sun in 9th House

Benefic:

(1) Native will be lucky, good natured will have good family life and will always help others.
(2) If Mercury is in the 5th house, the native will have fortune after 34 years.

Malefic:

(1) Native will be evil and troubled by his brothers.
(2) Dis-favor from government and loss of reputation.

Remedial Measures:

(1) Never accept articles of silver as gifts or donation. Donate silver articles frequently.
(2) Ancestral pots and utensils of brass must be used and not sold.
(3) Avoid extreme anger and extreme softness.

Sun in 10th House

Benefic:

(1) Benefits and favors from government, good health and financially stronger.
(2) The native will get a government job and comforts of vehicles and servants.
(3) The native will always be suspicious about others.

Malefic:

(1) If the Sun is in the 4th house, the native's father will die in his childhood.
(2) If the Sun is in the 10th house and moon is in the 5th house the native will have a very short life.
(3) If the 4th house is without any planet, the native will be deprived of government favors and benefits.

Remedial Measures:

(1) Never wear blue or black clothes.
(2) Throwing a copper coin in a river or canal for 43 years will be highly beneficial.
(3) Abstain from liquor and meat.

Sun in 11th House

Benefic:

(1) If the native is vegetarian he will have three sons and will himself be head of the house and will get benefits from government.
(2) Malefic :
(3) The Moon is in the 5th house and the Sun is not expected by good planets, the will have a short life span.

Remedial Measures:

(1) Abstain from meat and wine.
(2) Keep almonds or radishes near the head of the bed and offer it in the temple next day for long life and children.

Sun in 12th House

Benefic:

(1) If Ketu in the 2nd house the native will earn wealth after 24 years and will have good family life.
(2) If Venus and Mercury are together their then one will benefit from business and the native will always have steady source of income.

Malefic:

(1) Native will suffer from depression, financial loss from machineries and will be punished by the government.
(2) If the other evil planet is in the 1st house, the native will not be able to sleep peacefully at night.

Remedial Measures:

(1) Native should always have a courtyard in his house.
(2) One should be religious and truthful.
(3) Keep a Chakki in the house.
(4) Always forgive your enemies.

GEM FOR SUN

RUBY

RED

Chapter Two

MOON

Effects and Remedies

As explained in the preceding issue, the Sun is regarded as the generator of power that gives spirit and life to all planets, the Moon is considered to be the conductor of power lent by Sun and rules over the lives of the beings on this earth. Sun represents individuality, whereas Moon shows one's personality.

Moon governs over impregnation, conception, birth of a child and the animal instinct. She represents mother, mother's family, grandmother, old women, horse, navigation, agricultural land, Lord Shiva, love, kindness, mental peace, heart, services rendered for other's welfare and the 4th house.

The Moon's effect comes up in the 16th, 51st and 86th year of the native and similarly its 1st cycle falls in the 24th year, the 2nd in the 49th year and the 3rd cycle falls in the 94th year of the native. The Jupiter, Sun and Mars are Moon's friends, whereas Saturn, Rahu and Ketu are inimical to her. For her protection, the Moon sacrifices her friendly planets—Sun, Mars or Jupiter. Moon is the Lord of 4th house, stands exalted in the 2nd house of Taurus and becomes debilitated in the 8th house of Scorpio. The Moon provides very good results if placed in houses 1, 2, 3, 4, 5, 7 and 9 whereas the 6th, 8th, 10th, 11th and 12th houses are bad for the Moon. The death of a domestic animal or a horse, drying up of a person's well or pond, the loss of the senses of touching and feeling are the signs of moon turning malefic.

The placement of the Ketu in the 4th house causes Maître Rein i.e. mother's debt. In such a situation pieces of silver of equal weight and size be collected from every member of the family and the same should be thrown together into the running water of a river. Consequently all the ill effects would be warded off.

GENERAL REMEDIES FOR PLANET MOON IN BRIEF

Moon:

(1) Prepare Milk Kheer.
(2) Place the kheer on a Fresh Butea monosperma leaf. This leaf is widely used in South India on which many people would like to have lunch.
(3) Make sure it's a full moon day.
(4) Stand under a coconut tree, hold the leaf with the milk dish towards the moon and recite Moon mantra thrice in mind.
(5) Distribute before consuming.

SPECIAL REMEDIES FOR PLANET MOON IN DETAIL

Moon in 1st House

In general, the 1st house belongs to Mars and Sun. When the moon is also placed therein, this house will come under the combined influences of the Mars, the Sun and the Moon i.e. all the 3 mutual friends will be treated as occupants of this house. The Sun and Mars will extend all friendly support to their natural friend Moon placed on the throne i.e. the ascendant house.

Such native will be soft-hearted and will inherit all the traits and qualities of his mother. He will be either the eldest brother or will certainly be treated so. As long as the native receives the blessings of his mother and keeps her happy, he will continue to rise and prosper in every way.

The things and the relatives as represented by Mercury, who is inimical to Moon, will prove harmful to the native, e.g., the sister-in-law and the green color will affect adversely. Hence it is better to keep away from them.

Burning milk (for making Khoya) or selling milk for profit would reduce or minimize the power of the Moon placed in the 1st house, which means that the native's life and property would be destroyed if he engages himself in such activities. Such a native should serve others with water and milk freely for long life and all round prosperity. Such a native will get a life of about 90 years and will be bestowed with honors and fame by the Govt.

Remedies

1. Do not marry between the age of 24 and 27 years, i.e., marry either before 24 years of age or after 27 years of age.
2. Do not build a house out of your earnings between 24 and 27 years of age.
3. Keep away from the green color and sister-in-law. Do not keep a silver pot or kettle with a snout (Toti) in it in the house.
4. Offer water to the roots of a Banyan tree whenever you can afford.

Additional Remedies are:

1. Insert copper nails on the four corners of your bed. Whenever crossing a river, always throw coins in it for the well fare of your children.
2. Always keep a silver utensil in your house.
3. Use Silver pots for drinking water or milk and avoid the use of glassware for the same.

Moon in 2nd House

The results of the 2nd house, when Moon is placed therein, will be influenced by Jupiter, Venus and the Moon, because this is the solid house, the permanent house of Jupiter and Venus is the lord of the second Sign Taurus. The Moon gives very good results in this house, as it becomes very strong here because of the friendly support of Jupiter against Venus.

Such a native may not have sisters, but will certainly be having brothers. In case he doesn't have, his wife will certainly have brothers. He will certainly receive his due share in parental properties. Whatever be the planetary position otherwise, but the Moon here will ensure male offspring to the native.

The native will receive good education, which will add to his fortune. The Business associated with the things of the Moon will prove highly advantageous. He may be a reputed teacher also.

The Ketu placed in the 12th house will cause eclipse of the Moon here, which will deprive the native either of good education or of male children.

Remedies

(1) Temple within the native's house may deprive the native of male issue.
(2) The things associated with the Moon, i.e., silver, rice, non-cemented floor of the house, the mother and old women and their blessings will prove very lucky for the native.
(3) Offering green color clothes to small girls continuously for 43 days.
(4) Place the things associated with the Moon into the foundation of your house, e.g., a square piece of silver.

Moon in 3rd House

The results of the 3rd house, when the Moon is placed therein, will be influenced by the Mars, Mercury and Moon. Here the Moon proves highly beneficial to ensure a long life and great wealth or riches for the native.

If there are no planets in the 9th and 11th houses, then Mars and Venus will give good results to the native because of the Moon being in the 3rd house.

With the advancement of the native's education and learning, the economic condition of his father will deteriorate, but without affecting his education adversely. If dragon's tail placing in the horoscope is auspicious and not harming the Moon in the 3rd, the education of the native will bear good fruits and prove advantageous in every manner.

If the Moon is malefic, it will cause great loss of wealth and money at the age of the malefic planet placed in the 9th house.

Remedies

1. Offer in donation the things associated with the Moon, e.g., silver or rice, after the birth of a daughter and the things associated with the Sun e.g., wheat and jaggery when a son is born.
2. Do not make use of your daughter's money and wealth.
3. To avoid the evil effects of a malefic planet in the 8th house, serve the guests and others by offering them milk and water freely.

4. Worshipping Goddess Durga and obtaining the blessings of small girls by touching their feet after serving them food and sweets.

Moon in 4th House

The results of the 4th house are the general product of the total influences of Moon, the lord of the 4th Rashi Cancer and the permanent resident of the 4th house. Here the Moon becomes very strong and powerful in every manner.

The use of, and association with the things represented by the Moon will prove highly beneficial to the native. Offer milk in place of water to the guests. Obtain blessings of your mother or the elderly women by touching their feet. The 4th house is the river of income which will continue to increase expenditure. In other words, expenditure will augment income.

The native will be a reputed and honored person with soft heart and all sorts of riches. He will inherit all the traits and qualities of his mother and will face the problems of life boldly like a lion. He will receive honor and favors from the government along with riches and will provide peace and shelter to others.

Good education will be ensured for the native. If Jupiter is placed in the 6th house and Moon in the 4th, parental profession will suit him. If a person has mortgaged certain valuables to the native, he will never come back to demand it.

If Moon be placed with 4 planets in the 4th house, the native will be economically very strong and wealthy. The male planets will help the native like sons and the female planets like daughters.

Remedies

1. Selling of milk for profit and burning of milk for making Khoya, etc., will have a very adverse effects on income, life span and mental peace.
2. Adultery and flirtation will be seriously detrimental to the native's reputation and prospects of wealth gains. The more the expenses, the more the income.

3. Before beginning any auspicious or new work, place a pitcher or any container filled with milk in the house.
4. For warding off the evil generated by the Jupiter placed in the 10th house, the native should visit places of worship along with his grandfather and offer their oblations by placing their forehead at the feet of the deity.

Moon in 5th House

The results of the 5th house, when the Moon is placed therein, will be influenced by the Sun, the Ketu and the Moon. The native will adopt just and right means to earn wealth and will not yield to wrong doing. He may not do well in business but certainly receive favors and honors from the government. Anyone supported by him will win.

The Moon in the 5th house will give 5 sons if the Ketu is well placed and benefic even if the Moon is joined by malefic planets. By his education and learning the native will undertake several measures for others welfare, but the others will not do good to him.

Further, the native will be destroyed if he becomes greedy and selfish. If he fails to keep his plans a secret, his own men will damage him seriously.

Remedies

1. Keep control over your tongue. Never use abusive language to ward off troubles.
2. Avoid becoming greedy and over selfish.
3. Deceit and dishonesty towards others will affect you adversely.
4. Acting upon the advice of another person before trying to harm anybody will ensure very good results and a life of about 100 years.
5. Public service will enhance income and reputation of the native.

Moon in 6th House

This house is affected by the Mercury and Ketu. The Moon in this house will be affected by the planets placed in the 2nd, 8th, 12th and 4th houses. The native will receive education with obstacles and will have to struggle a lot for reaping the benefits of his educational achievements.

If the Moon is placed in the 6th, 2nd, 4th, 8th and 12th houses it is auspicious. The native would enliven a dying person by putting a few drops of water in his mouth.

But if the Moon is malefic in the 6th house and Mercury is placed in the 2nd or 12th house, the native will have suicidal tendencies. Similarly, if the Moon is malefic and the Sun is placed in the 12th house, then the native or his wife or both will have severe eye defects and troubles.

Remedies

1. Serve milk to your father with your own hands.
2. Never take milk during night. But intake of milk during day time and use of even curd and cheese during night is permissible.
3. Do not offer milk as donation. It can be given only at religious places of worship.
4. Digging of wells for public will destroy the issues, but digging of wells in a hospital or within the premises of cremation ground will not be harmful.

Moon in 7th house

The 7th house belongs to Venus and Mercury. When the Moon is placed here, the results of this house will be affected by the Venus, Mercury and Moon. Venus and Mercury combined together give the effects of the Sun. The 1st house aspects the 7th house. Consequently the rays of the Sun from the 1st house would be enlightening the Moon if placed in the 7th, which means that the things and the relatives represented by the Moon will provide highly beneficial and good results.

Educational achievements will prove fruitful for earning money or wealth. He may or may not have properties but will certainly have cash money in hand always. He will have good potential for being a poet or astrologer, or else he will be characterless and will have great love for mysticism and spiritualism.

The 7th Moon also denotes conflict between the native's wife and mother, adverse effects in milk trade. Disobedience towards mother will cause overall tensions and troubles.

Remedies

1. Avoid marriage in the 24th year of your life.
2. Always keep your mother happy.
3. Never sell milk or water for profit.
4. Do not burn milk for making Khoya.
5. Ensure that in marriage your wife brings silver and rice with her from her parents, equal to her weight.

Moon in 8th House

This house belongs to Mars and Saturn. The Moon here affects the education of the native adversely, but if education goes well the native's mother's life will be shortened and very often such a native loses both—education and the mother. However, the evil effects of the Moon in the 7th house will be mitigated if Jupiter and Saturn be placed in the 2nd house.

The 7th Moon often deprives the native of his parental properties. If there is a well or pond adjacent to the parental property of the native, he will receive adverse results of the Moon all through his life.

Remedies

1. Avoid gambling and flirting.
2. Perform shraddha ceremony for to your ancestors.
3. Do not build any house after covering a well with roof.
4. Obtain blessings of the old men and children by touching their feet.
5. Bring water from the well or water tap situated within the boundaries of a cremation ground and place it within your house. It will ward off all the evils generated by the Moon in the 7th house.
6. Offer gram and pulse in places of worship.

Moon in 9th House

The 9th house belongs to Jupiter, who is a great friend of the Moon. Hence the native will imbibe the traits and features of both these planets—good conduct, soft heartedness, religious bent of mind and love for virtuous acts and pilgrimage. He will live up to 75 years. A friendly planet in the 5th house will augment comforts and pleasures from the son and develops intense interest in religious deeds. A friendly planet in the 3rd house ensures great increase in money and wealth.

Remedies

1. Install the things associated with the Moon within the house, e.g., place a square piece of silver in the Amirah.
2. Serve the laborers with milk.
3. Offer milk to snakes and rice to fish.

Moon in 10th House

The 10th house is in every manner ruled by Saturn. This house is expected by the 4th house, which is similarly ruled by Moon. Hence the Moon in the 10th house ensures a long life of about 90 years for the native. Moon and Saturn are inimical, therefore, medicines in liquid form will always prove harmful to him. The milk will act as poison if taken during night. If he is a medical practitioner, dry medicines administered by him to the patient will have a magical effect for cure. If a surgeon, he will earn great wealth and fame for surgery. If the 2nd and 4th houses are empty money and wealth will rain on him.

If Saturn is placed in the 1st house, the native's life will be destroyed by the opposite sex, especially a widow.

The things and business represented by Saturn will prove beneficial for the native.

Remedies

1. Visits to religious places of worship will enhance the fortune of the native.
2. Store the natural water of rain or the river in a container and keep it within your house for 15 years. It will wash off the poisons and evil effects generated by the Moon in the 10th house.
3. Avoid taking milk during night.
4. Low animals can neither live long in your house nor will they prove beneficial or auspicious.
5. Abstain from wine, meat and adultery.

Moon in 11th house

This house is strongly influenced by Jupiter and Saturn. Every planet placed in this house will destroy its inimical planets and the things associated with them. In this way the Moon here will destroy its enemy Ketu's things, i.e., the sons of the native. Here the Moon will have to face the combined power of its enemies Saturn and Ketu, which will weaken the Moon. Now if Ketu is placed in the 4th house, the life of the native's mother will be endangered. The business associated with Mercury will also prove harmful. Starting house construction or purchase of a house on Saturdays will strengthen the Saturn (the Moon's enemy) which will prove disastrous for the native. Kanyadan after the midnight and participating in any marriage ceremony on Fridays will damage the fortunes of the native.

Remedies

1. Offer milk in Bhairo Baba"s Mandir and donate milk to others liberally.
2. Ensure that the grandmother does not see her grandson.
3. Heat up a piece of gold in fire and put it in a glass of milk before drinking it.
4. Throw 125 pieces of sweet (Peda) in a river.

Moon in 12th house

This house belongs to Moon's friend Jupiter. Here the Moon will have good effects on Mars and the things associated with Mars, but it will harm its enemies Mercury and Ketu and the things associated with them. Hence the business and things associated with the house in which Mars is placed will provide highly beneficial effects. Similarly, the business and things associated with the houses where Mercury and Ketu are placed will be strongly damaged. The Moon in the 12th houses causes a general fear in the native's mind about numerous unforeseen troubles and dangers and thus destroys his sleep and peace of mind. Ketu in the 4th house will become weak and affect the native's son and mother very adversely.

Remedies

1. Wearing Gold in ears, drinking milk after inserting hot piece of gold in it and visiting religious places of worship will ward off the evils of the Moon in 12th house and also that of the Ketu in the 4th house.
2. Never offer milk and food to religious saints/sadhus.
3. Do not open a school, college or any other educational institute and do not help children in obtaining free of cost education.

GEM FOR MOON

PEARL

WHITE

Chapter Three

MARS

Effects and Remedies

Mars is a dry, red and fiery planet. Masculine by nature it signifies energy, both constructive and destructive depending upon his position as Mars positive and Mars negative. If Sun and Mercury are placed together in one house, Mars would be positive but if Saturn and Sun are placed in one house Mars becomes negative.

Mars acts on the extremes—either soft like a wax or hard like a stone. The Sun, Moon and Jupiter are his friends, whereas Mercury and Ketu are his enemies. Rahu and Saturn are neutral to Mars. The first cycle of Mars runs between the ages 28 and 33, the 2nd between 63 and 68 years and the 3rd between 98 and 103 years. The 1st and 8th houses are the town houses of Mars and he gets exalted in the 10th house of his debilitation. Mars acts as a malefic in the 4th and 8th houses, but he is benefic if placed in the 1, 2, 3, 5, 6, 7, 9, 10, 11 and 12th houses.

Mars is the signification of sex, brothers, land and property and rules over the animal instincts in man. A benefic Mars offers self-confidence, sharp wit, faculty of argumentation and adventurous spirit, strong determination and qualities of leadership in all human pursuits. On the contrary, a weak and afflicted Mars makes the native lose temper quickly, fool hardy, quarrelsome and brutal. Such a Mars makes the native a sexual pervert.

GENERAL REMEDIES FOR PLANET MARS IN BRIEF

The general effects and remedial measures of Mars according to Lal Kitab is follows :

Mars:

1. Prepare Rice Starch dish, add some salt and red pepper [paprika]
2. Stand on a rock/mountain.
3. Hold the dish in your hands and recite Mars mantra.
4. Distribute before consuming.

SPECIAL REMEDIES FOR PLANET MARS IN DETAIL

Mars in 1st House

Mars in the 1st house makes the native good natured, truthful and richer from the 28th year of age. He wins favors from the government and victory against the enemies without much effort. He earns large profits from the business associated with Saturn i.e., iron, wood, machinery etc. and the relatives represented by Saturn i.e., nephews, grandsons, uncles etc.

Spontaneous curses from the mouth of such a native will never go waste. Association of Saturn with Mars provides physical trouble to the native.

Remedies

1. Avoid the acceptance of things free of cost or in charity.
2. Avoid evil deeds and telling lies.
3. Association with saints and Faqirs will prove very harmful.
4. Things of ivory will give very adverse effects. Avoid them.

Mars in 2nd House

The native with Mars in the 2nd house is generally the eldest issue of his parents, or else he or she would always like to be treated so. But living and behaving like a younger brother would prove highly beneficial and ward off several evils automatically. Mars in this house provides great wealth and properties from the in-laws' family. Mars negative here makes the native a snake in disguise for others and causes his death in war or quarrels.

Mars with Mercury in the 2nd house weakens the will power and undermines the importance of the native.

Remedies

1. The business associated with Moon, e.g., trade in cloth, will provide great prosperity, hence strengthen Moon.
2. Ensure that your in-laws make arrangements for providing drinking water facilities to the common people.
3. Keep deer skin in the house.

Mars in 3rd House

The 3rd house is affected by Mars and Mercury, who provide brothers and sisters to the native i.e., he will not be the only issue of his parents. Others will be highly benefited from the native, but he will not be able to receive benefit from others. Humbleness will bring rewards. In-laws will become richer and richer after the native's marriage. The native believes in the principle "eat, drink and be merry" and suffers from blood disorders.

Remedies

1. Be soft hearted and avoid arrogance. Be good to brothers for prosperity.
2. Keep articles of ivory with you.
3. Put on silver ring in the left hand.

Mars in 4th House

The 4th house is overall the property of Moon. The fire and heat of Mars in this house burns the cold water of Moon i.e., the properties of the Moon are adversely affected. The native loses peace of mind and suffers from jealousy to others. He always misbehaves with his younger brothers. The native's evil mission gets strong destructive powers. Such a native affects the life of his mother, wife, mother-in-law etc. very adversely. His anger becomes the cause of his overall destruction in various aspects of life.

Remedies

1. Offer sweet milk to the roots of a banyan tree and put that wet soil on your navel.
2. To avoid havoc from fire, place empty bags of sugar on the roof of your house, shop or factory.
3. Always keep a square piece of silver with you.
4. Keep away from black, one-eyed or disabled person.

Mars in 5th House

The 5th house belongs to the Sun, who is a natural friend of Mars. Hence Mars ensures very good results in this house. The sons of the native become instruments of wealth and fame for him. His prosperity increases manifold after the birth of sons. The things and relatives represented by Venus and Moon will prove beneficial in every manner. Someone of his forefathers must have been a doctor or Vaidya.

The prosperity of the native will continue to grow more and more with the growth in age. But romance and emotional affairs with the opposite sex will prove highly disastrous for the native, which will destroy his mental peace and night sleep too.

Remedies

1. Maintain a good moral character.
2. Keep water in a pot below the head side of your bed at night and drop it in a flower pot in the morning.
3. Offer Shraddha to your ancestors and plant a Neem tree in the house.

Mars in 6th House

This house belongs to Mercury and Ketu. Both are mutual enemies and inimical to Mars also. Hence Mars in this house will keep himself away from both. The native will be courageous, adventurous, lover of justice and powerful enough to set fire into water. He will be highly benefited by the trade and business associated with Mercury. His pen will wield more power than the sword. If Sun, Saturn and Mars are placed together in one house, the brothers, mother, sisters and wife will be affected very adversely.

Remedies

1. Distribute salt in place of sweets on the birth of a male child.
2. His brothers should keep the native happy by offering him something or the other for their protection and prosperity. But if he does not accept such things, the same should be thrown in water.
3. The male children of the native should not wear gold.
4. Adopt remedies of Saturn for family comfort. Worship Ganeshji for parents' health and destruction of enemies.

Mars in 7th House

This house belongs to the influences of Venus and Mercury, who combined together provide the effect of Sun. If Mars is placed therein, the 7th house will be affected by Sun and Mars both, which ensures that the native's ambition will be fulfilled. Wealth, property and family will increase.

But if Mercury is also placed here along with Mars, very adverse results will follow regarding the things and relations represented by Mercury e.g., sister, sister-in-law, nurses, maid servant, parrot, goats etc. Hence it would be better to keep away from them.

Remedies

1. Place solid piece of silver in the house for prosperity.
2. Always offer sweets to daughter, sister, sister-in-law and widows.
3. Repeatedly build a small wall and destroy it.

Mars in 8th House

The 8th house belongs to Mars and Saturn, who jointly influence the properties of this house. No planet is considered good in this house. Mars here affects very adversely the younger brothers of the native. The native sticks to commitments made by him without caring for profit or loss.

Remedies

1. Obtain blessings of widows and wear a silver chain.
2. Offer sweet loaves of bread prepared on Tandoor to dogs.
3. Take your meals in the kitchen.
4. Build a small dark room at the end of your house and do not allow sun light to enter it.
5. Offer rice, jaggery and gram pulse at religious places of worship.
6. Fill an earthen pot with 'Deshi Khand' and bury it near a cremation ground.

Mars in 9th House

This house belongs to Jupiter, a friend of Mars. Mars placed in this house will prove good in every manner to the native by virtue of the help and blessings of the elders. His brother's wife proves very fortunate for him. Generally he will have as many brothers as his father had. Living with brothers in a joint family will enhance all round happiness. The native will gain a highly prestigious administrative post upto the 28th year of his age. He may earn large profits in the trade of goods associated with warfare.

Remedies

1. Obedience to elder brother.
2. Render services to your Bhabhi i.e., brother's wife.
3. Do not become an atheist and follow your traditional customs and rituals.
4. Offer rice, milk and jaggery at religious places of worship.

Mars in 10th House

This is the best position of Mars in a horoscope, the place of his exaltation. If the native is born in a poor family, his family will become rich and affluent after his birth. If he is born in a rich family, his family will grow richer and richer after his birth. If the native is the eldest brother he will gain a more distinct recognition and reputation in society. He will be bold, courageous, healthy and competent enough to set traditions, norms and rules in society. However, if malefic planets Rahu, Ketu and Saturn or Venus and Moon are placed in the 2nd house, the aforesaid beneficial effects are reduced. Further if a friendly planet is placed in the 3rd house, it will also affect the results of Mars in the 10th house adversely. If Saturn is placed in the 3rd house, the native will gain huge wealth and large properties in the later part of his life along with a kingly position. Mars in the 10th house but no planet in the 5th house provides all round prosperity and happiness.

Remedies

1. Do not sell ancestral property and gold of the house.
2. Keep a pet deer in your house.
3. While boiling milk, please ensure that it should not overflow and fall on the fire.
4. Offer help to one-eyed and childless persons.

Mars in 11th House

Mars gives good results in this house, because this house is influenced by Jupiter and Saturn. If Jupiter is in exalted position, Mars gives very good results. Native is courageous and just and usually a trader.

Remedies

1. One should never sell one's ancestral property.
2. Keeping Sindoor or honey in an earthen pot will give good results.

Mars in 12th House

This house is inhabited by Jupiter, so now both Mars and Jupiter will give good results. This is also considered as the "solid house" of Rahu, so now Rahu will not trouble the native notwithstanding its position in native's horoscope.

Remedies

1. Take honey the first thing in the morning.
2. Eating sweets and offering sweets to another person will increase the wealth of the native.

GEM FOR MARS IS

CORAL

RED

Chapter Four

RAHU

Effects and Remedies

Unlike other planets of the solar system Rahu and Ketu are not observable, substantial heavenly bodies, with shape or mass content. Rightly termed as shadowy planets, their movement is interrelated and as parts of one body they are at all times just opposite to each other . Greater significance has been attached to the role of Rahu influencing human affairs in various dimensions, especially in Kalyug

The author of Lal Kitab describes Saturn as a serpent and Rahu and Ketu as its head and tail respectively. As a node of moon, Rahu shall not provide adverse results so long as 4th house or moon is not afflicted. He gives good results when Mars occupies houses 3 and 12, or when Sun and Mercury are in house 3, or when he himself is posited in 4th house. Rahu further provides good results if placed together with Mercury or expected by him.

Rahu offers highly beneficial effects if placed in houses earlier than Saturn. But if it is otherwise, Saturn becomes stronger and Rahu acts as his agent. Sun provides very good results when Rahu is expected by Saturn, but Rahu gives the effects of a debilitated planet when Saturn is expected by Rahu.

Rahu gets exalted in houses 3 and 6, whereas he gets debilitated in houses 8, 9 and 11. 12th house is his solid home and he proves highly auspicious in houses 3,4 and 6. Saturn, Mercury and Ketu are his friends, whereas Sun, Mars and Venus are his enemies. Jupiter and moon are neutral to him.

If Sun and Venus are placed together in a horoscope, Rahu will generally provide adverse results. Similarly, Rahu will provide bad results if Saturn and Sun are also combined in a horoscope. Here Mars will also become Mars

31

negative. If Ketu is placed in houses earlier than Rahu, Rahu will provide adverse results, whereas Ketu's effect would be zeroed.

Rahu:

GENERAL REMEDIES FOR PLANET RAHU IN BRIEF

1. Prepare Urad daal rice (vigna mungo/black gram)
2. Place it on a dry Butea monosperma leaf. This leaf is widely used in South India on which many people would like to have lunch.
3. Stand in a dry/barren/grass free land or near anthills.
4. Place the rice on the leaf, hold it in your hand and recite Rahu Mantra/sloka.
5. Distribute before consuming.

SPECIAL REMEDIES FOR PLANET RAHU IN DETAIL

Rahu in 1st House

1st house is influenced by Mars and Sun, which is like a throne. The planet in 1st house is considered to be the king of all planets.

The native will achieve a position higher than indicated by his qualification and will obtain good results from government. Rahu in this house would give the result of exalted Sun, but it will spoil the fruits of the house in which Sun is placed. If Mars, Saturn and Ketu are weak only then Rahu would give bad results, otherwise it will give good results in 1st house. If Rahu is malefic the native should never take any electric equipment's or blue/black clothes from his in-laws, else his son could be affected adversely. its malefic result too could last till the age of 42 years.

Remedies

1. Offer 400 gm lead in running water .
2. Wear silver in the neck.
3. Mix barley in milk in ratio of 1:4 and offer in running water.
4. Offer coconut in running water.

Rahu in 2nd House

If Rahu is in benefic form in 2nd house one gets money, prestige and lives like a king. He will have a long life. 2nd house is influenced by Jupiter and Venus. If Jupiter is benefic then the native will live the early years of his life in wealth and comfort. If Rahu is malefic the native will be poor and have a bad family life, suffer from intestinal disorders. The native is killed by a weapon and is unable to save money. In the 10th, 21st to 42nd years of his life, he loses wealth by theft etc.

Remedies

1. Keep a solid silver ball in the pocket.
2. Wear things associated with Jupiter, like gold, yellow cloth, saffron etc.
3. Keep cordial relations with ones mother.
4. After marriage do not take any electric equipment from in-laws.

Rahu in 3rd House

It is the solid house of Rahu. 3rd house belongs to Mercury and is influenced by Mars. When Rahu is benefic the native will enjoy great wealth and a long life. He will be fearless and a loyal friend. He would be a clairvoyant for seeing future in his dreams. He will never be issueless. He will be victorious over his enemies; can never be a debtor. He would leave behind property. 22nd year of his life would be of progress. However if Rahu is malefic in 3rd house then his brothers and relatives would waste his money. His money once borrowed would never be returned. He would have defective speech and would be an atheist. If Sun and Mercury are also there (in 3rd house) with Rahu then his sister would become a widow in 22nd or 32nd year of his life.

Remedies

1. Never keep ivory or things of ivory in the house.

Rahu in 4th House

This house belongs to moon, which is an enemy of Rahu. When Rahu is benefic in this house the native would be intelligent, wealthy and will spend money on good things. Going on pilgrimage would be beneficial for him. If Venus is also benefic then after marriage the native's in-laws could also become rich and the native would also benefit from them.

When Moon is exalted the native would become very rich and would benefit from the works or relatives associated with Mercury. If Rahu is malefic and the Moon is also weak then the native will suffer from poverty and native's mother would also suffer. Collecting char coal, altering toilet, installing oven in the ground and alteration of the roof in the house would be indicative of malefic.

Remedies

1. Wear silver.
2. Offer 400 gm coriander or almonds, or both in flowing water.

Rahu in 5th House

5th house belongs to Sun, which signifies male offspring. If Rahu is benefic native will be rich, wise, enjoy good health. He would enjoy good income and good progress. The native would be a devout or philosopher. If Rahu is malefic it leads to abortions. After the birth of a son, wife's health will suffer for twelve years. If Jupiter is also in 5th house father of native will be in trouble.

Remedies

1. Keep an elephant made of silver.
2. Abstain from wine, non-vegetarianism and adultery.
3. Remarry your wife.

Rahu in 6th House (Exalted)

This house is influenced by Mercury or Ketu. Here Rahu is exalted and gives very good results. The native will be free of all botherations or troubles.

The native will spend money on clothes. The native will be intelligent and victorious. When Rahu is malefic he will harm his brothers or friends. When mercury or Mars is in 12th house Rahu gives bad result. The native suffers from various ailments or loss of wealth. Sneezing while going to work would give bad results.

Remedies

1. Keep a black dog. Keep a lead nail in your pocket.
2. Never harm ones brothers/sisters.

Rahu in 7th House

Native will be rich, but wife would suffer. He would be victorious over his enemies. If the marriage takes place before twenty one years, it would be inauspicious. He would have good relations with the government. But if he engages in business connected with Rahu, like electrical equipment's, then he will have losses. Native would suffer from head ache and if Mercury, Venus or Ketu is in 11th house, then sister, wife or son would destroy the native.

Remedies

1. Never marry before 21st year of age.
2. Offer six coconuts in river.

Rahu in 8th House

8th house is concerned with Saturn and Mars. So Rahu in this house gives malefic effect. The native would spend money uselessly on court cases. Family life would be adversely affected. If Mars is benefic and is placed in 1st or 8th house or Saturn (benefic) is placed in 8th house, the native will be very rich.

Remedies

1. Keep a square piece of silver.
2. While sleeping Saunf should be keep under the pillow.
3. Do not work in electricity or power department.

Rahu in 9th House

9th house is influenced by Jupiter. If the native has good relation with ones brothers and sisters it is fruitful; else it would adversely affect the native. If the native is not religious minded then his progeny would be useless for him. Professions influenced by Saturn would be profitable.

If Jupiter is in 5th or 11th house then it is useless. If Rahu is inauspicious in 9th house then chances of begetting a son are less, especially if native files court cases against one's blood relation. Rahu is in 9th and 1st house is empty then health could be adversely affected and one gets insulted and mental problems, especially from orders. Remedies

1. Use Tilak of saffron daily.
2. Wear gold.
3. Always keep a dog (it saves ones progeny).
4. Have good relations with your in-laws.

Rahu in 10th House

Keeping one's head uncovered gives the effect of a debilitated Rahu in 10th house. The good or bad result of Rahu would depend upon Saturn's position. If Saturn is auspicious then native would be brave, long lived and rich and get respect from all quarters. If Rahu in 10th house is with Moon it gives Raja Yoga. The native is lucky for one's father. If Rahu in 10th house is malefic then it would adversely affect ones mother or native's health would also be bad. If Moon is alone in 4th house then native's eyes are adversely affected. He suffers from headaches and there is loss of wealth, because of a dark complexioned person.

Remedies

1. Use blue or black cap.
2. Cover one's head.
3. Offer 4kg. or 400 gms of 'sugar' in a temple, or in flowing water.
4. Feed blind people.

Rahu in 11th House

11th house is influenced by both Saturn and Jupiter. Native could be rich as long as his father is alive. Alternatively, establishing things of Jupiter would help.

Native has wicked friends. He gets money from mean people. After the death of ones father he should wear gold in the neck. If Mars is malefic for a native with Rahu in 11th at time of his birth, there is everything in his house, but all gets destroyed later. If Rahu in 11th house is malefic then the native has bad relations with his father or he may even kill him. Planet in 2nd house would act as enemy. If Jupiter/Saturn are in 3rd or 11th house then wear iron on the body and drink water in a silver glass. If Ketu is in 5th house then Ketu gives bad results. There may be diseases of ear, spine, urinary problems etc. There may be losses associated with business concerned with Ketu.

Remedies

1. Wear iron. Use silver glass for drinking water.
2. Never take any electric equipment as a gift.
3. Do not keep blue sapphire, ivory or toys in the shape of an elephant.

Rahu in 12th House

12th house belongs to Jupiter. It signifies bedroom. Rahu here gives mental troubles, insomnia. It also leads to excessive expenditure on sisters and daughters. If Rahu is with its enemies then it becomes next to impossible to make ends meet, despite hard labor. It also leads to false allegations. One may even go to the extreme of contemplating suicide. One has mental worries.

Telling lies, deceiving others etc. may make Rahu even more malefic. If somebody sneezes at the start of any new work if gives malefic effect. There may be theft, diseases or false allegations. If mars is with Rahu here, then it gives good results.

Remedies

1. Take your meals in the kitchen itself.
2. Keep Saunf and khand under the pillow for good night's sleep.

GEM FOR RAHU

GOMED

MAROON

Chapter Five

JUPITER

Effects and Remedies

Jupiter is a fiery, noble, benevolent, masculine, expansive, optimistic, positive and dignified planet. higher attributes of the mind and soul, generosity, joy, jubilation and joviality along with high reasoning ability and the power of right judgments are all governed by Jupiter.

Jupiter rules educational interests, law, religion, philosophy, banking, and economics and indicates the extent of one's love and longing for religion, scriptures, elders and preceptors. He is also a signification of wealth, progress, philosophic nature, good conduct, health and children.

Jupiter represents 'Thursday' and the yellow color. He is regarded as 'Karaka' for 2nd, 5th and 9th houses. The sun, mars and moon are his friends, whereas Mercury and Venus are enemies to him. Rahu, Ketu and Saturn adopt neutrality to him. He stands exalted in the 4th house and the 10th house is the house of his debilitation.

Jupiter provides good results if placed in houses 1, 5, 8, 9 and 12, but 6th, 7th and the 10th are the bad houses for him. Jupiter gives bad results when Venus or Mercury get placed in the 10th house of a horoscope. However, Jupiter never gives bad results if placed alone in any house. A malefic Jupiter affects the Ketu (son) very adversely. Jupiter offers malefic results if he is placed with Saturn, Rahu or Ketu in a horoscope.

GENER REMEDIES FOR PLANET JUPITER IN BRIEF

For Jupiter: Offer curd rice in a silver dish to Load Shiva on Thursday and distribute it poor people or family members before you consume. Make sure curd is not too sweet.

SPECIAL REMEDIES FOR PLANET JUPITER IN DETAIL

Jupiter in 1st House

Jupiter in the 1st house makes the native necessarily rich, even if he is deprived of learning and education. He will be healthy and never afraid of enemies. He will rise every 8th year of his life through his own efforts and with the help of friends in the government. If the 7th house is not occupied by any planet success and prosperity will come after the marriage of the native. Marriage or construction of a house with one's own earnings in the 24th or 27th year would prove inauspicious for the longevity of the father's life. Jupiter in 1st house along with the Saturn in the 9th house causes health problems for the native.

Jupiter in the first house and Rahu in the 8thcauses the death of the native's father because of heart attack or asthma.

Remedies

1. Offer the things of mercury, Venus and Saturn to the religious places.
2. Serving cows and helping untouchables.
3. If Saturn is placed in the 5th house, don't build a house.
4. If Saturn is placed in the 9th house, don't buy machinery associated with Saturn.
5. If Saturn is in 11th or 12th house, avoid use wine, meat and eggs strictly.
6. Ward-off the evil effects of mercury by putting on silver in the nose.

Jupiter in 2nd House

The results of this house are affected by Jupiter and Venus as if they are together in this house, though Venus may be placed anywhere in the chart. Venus and

Jupiter are inimical to each other. Hence both will affect each other adversely. Consequently, if the native engages himself in the trade of gold or jewelry, then the things of Venus like wife, wealth and property will get destroyed.

As long as the wife of the native is with him, the native will continue gaining honor and wealth despite the fact that his wife and her family may be suffering because of ill health and other problems. The native is admired by females and inherits the property of his father. He may be benefited by lottery or property of a person having no issues, if the 2nd, 6th and 8th houses are auspicious and Saturn is not placed in the 10th.

Remedies

1. Charity and donations will ensure prosperity.
2. Offer milk to snakes for warding off the evils of Saturn placed in the 10th.
3. Fill up the pits if any on the road side, in front of your house.

Jupiter in 3rd House

The Jupiter in the 3rd house makes the native learned and rich, who receives continuous income from the government all through his life. Saturn in the 9th makes the native live long, whereas if Saturn is placed in the 2nd the native becomes extremely clever and crafty. However Saturn is the 4th indicates that the native will be robbed of money and wealth by his friends. If Jupiter is accompanied by inimical planets in the 3rd the native is destroyed and becomes a liability on his closer ones.

Remedies

(1) Worship of Goddess Durga and offering sweets and fruits to small girls and obtaining their blessing by uching their feet. Avoid sycophants.

Jupiter in 4th House

The 4th house belongs to Moon, a friend of Jupiter, who stands exalted in this house. Hence Jupiter here gives very good results and provides the native the powers of deciding the fate and fortune of others. He will possess money, wealth and large properties along with honor and favors from the government. In times of crisis the native will receive divine help. As he grows old his prosperity and money will increase. How so ever if he has built a temple at home Jupiter will not give the above mentioned results and the native will have to face poverty and disturbed married life.

Remedies

1. The native should not keep a temple in his house.
2. He should serve his elders.
3. He should offer milk to snake.
4. He should never bare his body before anyone.

Jupiter in 5th House

This house belongs to Jupiter and sun. Native's prosperity will increase after the birth of his son. In fact, more sons a native has, the more prosperous he will become. 5th house is the own house of Surya and in this house Surya, Ketu and Brihaspati will give mixed results. However if Mercury, Venus and Rahu is in 2nd, 9th, 11th or 12th houses then Jupiter sun and Ketu will give bad results. If the native is honest and laborious then Jupiter will give good results.

Remedies

1. Do not accept any donations or gifts.
2. Offers your services to priests and sadhus.

Jupiter in 6th House

6th house belongs to Mercury and Ketu also has its effect on this house. so this house will give combined effects of Mercury, Jupiter and Ketu. If Jupiter is benefic the native will be of pious nature. He will get everything in life without asking. Donations and offerings in the name of elders will prove beneficial. If Jupiter is in 6th and Ketu is benefic then native will become selfish. However, if Ketu is malefic in 6th house and mercury is also malefic the native will be unlucky up to 34 years of age. Here Jupiter causes asthma to the native's father

Remedies

1. Offer things connected with Jupiter in a temple.
2. Feed the cocks.
3. Offer clothes to the priest.

Jupiter in 7th House

7th house belongs to Venus, so it will give mixed results. The native will have rise in luck after marriage and native will be involved in religious works. The good result of the house will depend upon position of moon. The native will never be a debtor and will have good children. And if the sun is also in 1st house the native will be a good astrologer and lover of comforts.

However if Jupiter is malefic in 7th house and Saturn is in the 9th the native will become a thief. If mercury is in the 9th then his married life will be full of problems. If Jupiter is malefic native will never get support from brothers and will be deprived of favors from the government. Jupiter in 7th house causes differences with the father. If so one should never donate clothes to anyone, otherwise one will certainly get reduced to extreme poverty.

Remedies

1. Offer worship to lord Shiva.
2. One should not keep idols of god in one's house.
3. Keep gold tied in a yellow cloth always with you.
4. One should stay away from yellow clad sadhus and saints.

Jupiter in 8th House

Jupiter does not give good results in this house, but one will get all the worldly comforts. In the time of distress, one will get help from god. Being religious will increase native's luck. As long as the native is wearing gold he will not be unhappy or ill. If there is Mercury, Venus or Rahu in 2nd, 5th, 9th, 11th and 12th house, native's father will be ill and native himself will face loss of prestige.

Remedies

1. Offer things connected with Rahu, like wheat, barley, coconut into running water.
2. Plant a pipal tree in a cremation ground.
3. Offer ghee and potatoes and camphor in temple.

Jupiter in 9th House

9th house is especially influenced by Jupiter. so the native will be famous, rich and will be born in a rich family. The native will be true to his words and will have long life and have good children. In case Jupiter is malefic the native will have none of these qualities and will be atheistic. If the native has any planet inimical to Jupiter in the 1st, 5th and 4th house then Jupiter will give bad results.

Remedies

1. One should go to temple everyday
2. Abstain from drinking alcohol.
3. Offer rice to running water.

Jupiter in 10th House

This house belongs to Saturn. So the native will have to imbibe the qualities of Saturn only then he will be happy. the native should be cunning and sly. only then the can enjoy the good results of Jupiter. If sun is in the 4th house Jupiter will give very good results. Venus and Mars in the 4th house ensure multi-marriages for the native. if friendly planets are placed in the 2nd, 4th and 6th houses, Jupiter provides highly beneficial results in matters of money and wealth. A malefic Jupiter in the 10th makes the native sad and impoverished. He is deprived of ancestral properties, wife and children.

Remedies

1. Clean your nose before beginning any work.
2. Throw copper coins in the running water of a river for 43 days.
3. Offer almonds to religious places.

4. A temple with idols must not be established within the house.
5. Put tilak of saffron on the forehead.

Jupiter in 11th House

Jupiter in this house affects the things and relatives of his enemies Mercury, Venus and Rahu very adversely. Consequently, the wife of the native will remain miserable. Similarly, sisters, daughters and father's sisters will also remain unhappy. The native will be a debtor even if mercury is well placed. The native will be comfortable only as long as his father lives with him in a joint family along with brothers, sisters and mother.

Remedies

1. Always keep gold on your body.
2. Put on a copper bangle.
3. Watering a pipal tree would prove beneficial.

Jupiter in 12th House

The 12th house would provide the combined influences of Jupiter and Rahu, who are inimical to each other. If the native observes good conduct, wishes good for all and observes religious practices he will become happy and enjoy a comfortable sleep at night. He would become wealthy and powerful. Abstaining from evil acts of Saturn will make the business of machinery, motor, trucks and cars highly beneficial to him.

Remedies

1. Avoid furnishing false evidence in any matter.
2. Render services to sadhus, pipal gurus and pipal tree.
3. Place water and Saunf on the head side of your bed during nights.

GEMS FOR JUPITER

YELLOW SAPPHIRE/TOPAZ

YELLOW

Chapter Six

SATURN

Effects and Remedies

As the slowest moving planet and the chief signification for longevity, Saturn is a barren, binding, cold, dry, hard, defensive and secretive planet. Its effects and influences are felt with greater intensity and for longer periods than any other planet. Saturn is considered to be very favorable for people born in the signs owned by Venus, whereas Saturn is evil to those born in the signs owned by Mercury.

The astrological thesis of Lal Kitab describes Saturn as a serpent, whose head or mouth is Rahu and Ketu is its tail. If ketu is posited in earlier houses than Saturn, the latter becomes a great benefit for the native. However, if the position is otherwise, the Saturn throws highest poisonous results on the native. Further, Saturn never gives malefic effects if posited in houses of Jupiter i.e. 2, 5, 9 or 12, whereas Jupiter provides bad results if posited in the house of Saturn.

Saturn is considered good in houses 2nd, 3rd and 7th to 12th, whereas 1st, 4th, 5th and 6th houses are bad for Saturn. Sun, Moon and Mars are its enemies, Venus, Mercury and Rahu are friends and Jupiter and Ketu are neutral to it. Saturn gets exalted in 7th house and the 1st house is the house of its debilitation. Venus and Jupiter placed together act like Saturn in that house. Similarly Mars and Mercury placed in a single house act like Saturn in that house. In the former case Saturn behaves like Ketu, while in the latter case it behaves like Rahu.

Venus gets destroyed if Saturn is being expected by the Sun in any horoscope. The aspect of Venus on Saturn causes loss of money and wealth, but the aspect of Saturn on Venus proves highly beneficial. Collision of Saturn and Moon causes operation of the eyes of the native. Saturn gives good results if posited in house earlier than sun.

Saturn can never give malefic results if posited with Sun or Jupiter in a single house, but highly adverse results would follow if posited with Moon or Mars in any house. Saturn releases its poisonous results on the sign and Mars, if it is posited in 1st house, on Mars only if posited in 3rd house, on moon if posited in 4th house, on sun if posited in 5th house, and on Mars in posited in 3rd house. Saturn in 3rd house deprives the native of the accumulation of cash money and kills the children of the native when posited in 5th house and 10th house is empty. It becomes highly benefic in 12th house if friendly planets are posited in 2nd house. Saturn provides very good results if placed in houses 1 to 7 on the condition that 10th house is empty.

Saturn in 1st house and sun in 7th, 10th or 11th houses causes all sorts of troubles for native's wife. Combination of Mars and Saturn gives adverse results al through.

GENERAL REMEDIES FOR PLANET SATURN IN BRIEF

Saturn (this will cancel out 95 to 100% negative effects)

1. Buy a 100% pure bronze dish with your own money—make sure there is no iron/copper mix [color].
2. Wash the dish; remove any labels or black spots.
3. Prepare till rice—do this just like you prepare any other dish, add salt and other ingredients if you want.
4. Ensure Saturn is in Libra, Capricorn or Aquarius in a non-retrograde state,
5. Mark the time when Saturn rises in your city on Saturday, some people will find this tricky . . . but you have to find out.
6. Light a lamp using till oil.
7. Place the till rice on the bronze dish and the lamp.
8. Go to the terrace of your house. Turn east and recite Saturn Mantra 19 times. Wait till the lamp runs out of oil.
9. Come downstairs, distribute till rice to all your family before you consume.
10. Use the same dish for lunch or dinner after that.
11. Saturn (this will cancel out 95 to 100% negative effects)

SPECIAL REMEDIES FOR PLANET SATURN IN DETAIL

Saturn in 1st House

1st house is influenced by Sun and Mars. Saturn in 1st house will give good results only when 3rd, 7th or 10th houses are not inhabited by any planet which is inimical to Saturn. If Mercury or Venus, Rahu or Ketu is in 7th house, Saturn will always give good results. In case Saturn is malefic and the native has a hairy body, the native will remain poor. If native celebrates his birthday it will give very bad results however the native will have a long life.

Remedies

1. Abstinence from alcohol and non-vegetarian meals.
2. Burying Surma in the ground will be beneficial for

1. Promotion in service and business.
2. Serving monkey will lead to prosperity.
3. Offering sweet milk to the roots of a banyan tree will give good results as regards education and health.

Saturn in 2nd House

The native will be wise, kind and just. He will enjoy wealth and will be of religious temperament. However, whether Saturn is benefic or malefic in this house, it will be decided by the planets placed in 8th house. The state of finance of the native will be decided by 7th house, the number of male members in the family by 6th house and age by 8th house. When Saturn is malefic in this house, after the native's marriage his in laws will face problems.

Remedies

1. Going barefoot to temple for forty three days.
2. Putting a tilak of curd or milk on the forehead.
3. Offering milk to snake.

Saturn in 3rd House

In this house Saturn gives good results. This house is the strong house of Mars. When Ketu aspects this house or is placed here Saturn will give very good results. The native will be healthy, wise and very intuitive. If the native is wealthy he will have few male members in the family and vice versa. As long as the native abstains from wine and non-vegetarianism, he will enjoy a long and healthy life.

Remedies

1. Serve three dogs.
2. Distributing medicines for eyes free.
3. Keeping a dark room in the house will prove highly beneficial.

Saturn in 4th House

This house belongs to Moon. So it will give mixed results in this house. The native will be devoted to his parents and will be of loving nature. Whenever the native is suffering from bad health, the use of things associated with Saturn will give good results. In native's family someone will be associated with medical profession.

When Saturn is malefic in this house drinking wine, killing of snakes and laying the foundation of the house at night will give very bad results. Drinking milk in the night will also give bad results.

Remedies

1. Offering milk to snake and offering milk or rice to crow or buffalo.
2. Pouring milk in the well.
3. Pouring rum in running water.

Saturn in 5th House

This house belongs to Sun, which is inimical to Saturn. The native will be proud. He should not construct a house till 48 years, otherwise his son will suffer. He should live in the house bought or constructed by his son. He should keep articles of Jupiter and Mars in his ancestral house for welfare of his children. If the native has hairy body, he will be dishonest.

Remedies

1. Distributing salty things while celebrating son's birthday.
2. Offering almonds in the temple and bringing and keeping half of it in the house.

Saturn in 6th House

If the work related to Saturn is done at night it will always give beneficial results. When marriage takes place after 28 years it will produce good results. when Ketu is well placed the native will enjoy wealth, profitable journey and happiness from children. When Saturn is malefic bringing things associated with Saturn, like leather and things of iron, will give bad results, especially when Saturn is in 6th house in varshaphal

Remedies

1. Serving a black dog and offering meals to it.
2. Offering coconut and almonds in the running water.
3. Serving snakes will prove advantageous for the welfare of children.

Saturn in 7th House

This house is influenced by Mercury and Venus, both friends of Saturn. so this planet gives very good results in this house. The professions associated with Saturn, like machinery and iron, will be very profitable. If the native maintains good relation with his wife, he will be rich and prosperous; will enjoy a long life and good health. If Jupiter is in 1st house, there will be gain from government.

Saturn becomes malefic if the native commits adultery and drinks wine. If the native gets married after 22 years his eyesight will be affected adversely.

Remedies

1. Bury a flute filled with sugar in a deserted place.
2. Serving black cow.

Saturn in 8th House

In 8th house no planet is considered auspicious. The native has a long life, but his father's life span is short and native's brothers turn out to be his foes. This house is considered headquarter of Saturn, but it will give bad result if Mercury, Rahu and Ketu are malefic in the native's horoscope.

Remedies

1. Keeping a square piece of silver.
2. Putting milk in water and sitting on a stone or wood while taking bath.

Saturn in 9th House

Native will have three houses. He will be a successful tour operator or civil engineer. He will enjoy a long and happy life and parents also will have a happy life. Maintaining three generations will protect from the bad effects of Saturn. if the native is helpful to others Saturn will always give good results. The native will have a son, though he will be born late.

Remedies

1. Offering rice or almonds in running water.
2. Work associated with Jupiter-gold, kiesar and Moon (silver cloth) will give good results.

Saturn in 10th House

This is Saturn's own house, where it will give good results. The native will enjoy wealth and property as long as he does not get a house constructed. Native will be ambitious and enjoy favors from government. The native should behave with shrewdness and should do his work while sitting at one place. only then he will enjoy the benefits of Saturn.

Remedies

1. Going to temple.
2. Abstinence from meat, wine and eggs.
3. Offering food to ten blind people.

Saturn in 11th House

Native's fate will be decided at the age of forty eight years. The native will never remain childless. Native will earn money by shrewdness and deceit. Saturn will give good or bad results according to the position of Rahu and Ketu

Remedies

1. Before going for an important work place a vessel filled with water and drop oil or wine on earth for forty three days.
2. Abstinence from drinking and maintaining good moral character.

Saturn in 12th House

Saturn gives good results in this house. Native will not have enemies. He will have many houses. His family and business will increase. He will be very rich. However Saturn will become malefic if the native starts drinking wine and becomes non-vegetarian, or if the dark room in the house is illuminated.

Remedies

1. Tying twelve almonds in a black cloth and placing it in a iron pot and keeping it in a dark room will give good results.

GEM FOR SATURN

1. NEELAM/BLUE-SAPPHIRE
2. BLUE

Chapter Seven

SADE SATI

SATURN'S
SEVEN AND HALF YEAR'S CYCLE

"Shani's-Sade-Sati"

A horoscope is said to be under

"Sade-Sati" effect when the Saturn transits through the 12th, 1st and 2nd house from natal Moon. It is said to be under "Daiya" effect when Saturn Transits over the 4th and 8th house over the natal Moon.

The Effect of "Sade-Sati" remain for seven and a half years and that Of "Daiya" remains for two and a half years.

This generally Effects health, mental peace and finance.

Generally "Sade-Sati" comes thrice in a horoscope in the lifetime. First in childhood, second in youth and Third in old age.

First "Sade-Sati" has effect on education & parents. Second "Sade-Sati" has effect on profession finance & family. The last one affects health than anything else.

Remedies of "Sade-Sati"

Generally the best remedy of "Sade-Sati" is to wear an iron ring made of a horse shoe or of a nail from a boat of a river or lake. There are many other remedies also according to the individual horoscope of a person. "Sade-Sati" is not malefic for all people it is benefic for those people for whom Saturn is a benefic.

After consultation with an astrologer a "Blue Sapphire or Neelam of can be worn to minimize the effect of Saturn

GEM FOR SATURN

NEELAM / BLUE-SAPPHIRE

BLUE

Chapter Eight

MERCURY

Effects and Remedies

In astrological parlance Mercury has been understood as an externally variable, vacillating, convertible, neutral and dualistic planet. Mercury reflects the mentality of an individual governs the reaction to our senses and impressions and rules over the central nervous system. As an intellectual planet it represents intelligence, genius, analytic power and reproducibility. Mercury is the smallest planet of the solar system. The author of Lal Kitab has compared mercury with a bat, which keeps hanging upside down and pounces upon the face of a child at the first opportunity. The native fails to understand anything and meanwhile the mysterious and mischievous mercury turns the cycle of fortune in the reverse gear. Mercury produces the effects of the planet or planets it is associated with. Mercury is considered malefic in the 3rd, 8th, 9th and 12th houses. Rahu gives bad results in 1, 5, 7, 8 and 11th houses.

If mercury and Rahu both are in their auspicious houses then Mercury causes havoc in the native's houses and produces disastrous result like putting the native behind the bars or creating troubles of the same sort. Mercury is considered auspicious in the 1, 2, 4, 5, 6 and the 7th houses and gives bad results when placed in the 3, 8, 9, 10, 11 and 12th. Its color is green and moon is its enemy. Sun Venus and Rahu are friends, whereas mars, Saturn, and Ketu are neutral to him. 7th house is the solid home of mercury. It stands exalted in the 6th house and gets debilitated in the 12th house. Affected Venus causes diseases of tooth and nervous system. If mercury is placed alone in any house the native keeps running and wasting time here and there.

GENERAL REMEDIES FOR PLANET MERCURY IN BRIEF

1. Prepare a Sweet dish made out of milk—such as milk peda. Do not buy.
2. Add lots of sugar
3. Place the dish on a fresh banana leaf. Avoid yellow, semi-dry leaves.
4. Stand in the lake/vacant place
5. Hold the leaf with the dish and recite Mercury mantra/sloka 7 times (in mind).
6. Give the sweets to children/students or those attending exams/interviews before consuming.

SPECIAL REMEDIES FOR PLANET MERCURY IN DETAIL

Mercury in 1st House

Mercury in 1st house makes the native kind, humorous and diplomatic with administrative skill. Such a native generally lives long and becomes selfish and mischievous by nature having special attraction for non-vegetarian dishes and drinks. He receives favor from the government and his daughters have royal and luxurious lives. The relatives represented by the house in which sun is placed gain wealth and riches within a little time and he himself will be having many sources of income. If Sun is placed along with Mercury in the 1st house or if the Mercury is expected by Sun the wife of native will come from a rich and noble family and will be good natured. Such a native will be affected by the evil effects of Mars but Sun will never give bad effects.

Rahu and Ketu will have evil effects, which suggest that the in laws and the offspring of the native will be adverse. If mercury is in the 1st house, the native will be adept in the art of influencing others and he will live like a king. Malefic Mercury in the 1st house along with Moon in the 7th house destroys the native because of intoxication.

Remedies

1. Keep away from the things of green color and sisters in law.
2. Avoid consumption of meat, eggs and liquor.

3. Business that requires your sitting at one place would be more beneficial
4. 206 than the one that requires running around.

Mercury in 2nd House

Mercury in the 2nd house makes the native intelligent self-centered, destroyer of enemies and cheats. He may be able to provide sufficient happiness to his father. he will be rich. The things represented by mars and Venus will prove beneficial to him.

Remedies

1. Abstain from eggs meat and liquor.
2. Association with your sisters in law is harmful.
3. Keeping sheep, goat and parrots as pets is strictly prohibited.

Mercury in 3rd House

Mercury in the 3rd house is not considered good. Mercury is inimical to Mars. But Mars does not have enmity with mercury. therefore the native could receive benefits from his brother, but he will not be beneficial to his brother or others. By virtue of its aspects of 9th and 11th houses Mercury affects the income and the condition of the father very adversely.

Remedies

1. Clean your teeth with alum every day.
2. Feed birds and donate a goat.
3. Don't live in a south facing house.
4. Distribute medicines of asthma.

Mercury in 4th House

The native in the 4th house is considered fortunate, very dear to his mother, good trader and receives favors from the government. However mercury in this house affects the income and health of another person adversely.

Remedies

1. Putting on silver chain for mental peace and golden chain for gaining wealth and property.
2. Putting Kiesar Tilak regularly for 43 days on fore—head.
3. Serving monkeys by offering jaggery.

Mercury in 5th house

Mercury in this house makes the native happy, wealthy and wise. Spontaneous utterances from the mouth of the native will certainly prove true.

It gives very good results if the moon or any male planet is placed in 3rd, 5th, 9th and 11th houses, but if moon and Jupiter are not placed in good houses mercury would provide malefic effects.

Remedies

1. Wear a copper coin in white thread for obtaining riches.
2. Serving cows for the happiness of wife and good luck.
3. A Gomukhi house (narrow at the front and wider at the end) would prove highly auspicious whereas Shermukhi
4. 211 house (wider at the front and narrower at the end) would prove highly disastrous.

Mercury in 6th House

Mercury becomes exalted in the 6th house. The native will be self-made man and will receive benefits from agricultural land, stationery, printing press and trade. Good or evil words from his mouth will never go waste. north facing house will give bad results. Daughter's marriage in the north direction will make her unhappy in every way.

Remedies

1. Burying a bottle filled with Ganga water into the agricultural land.
2. Putting on a silver ring in the left hand of one's wife.

3. Starting any important work in the presence of a girl or daughters or with flowers in hand proves auspicious.

Mercury in 7th House

In a male horoscope, mercury in the 7th house proves highly beneficial for others for whom the native wishes well. in a female horoscope it produces good result. The pen of the native wields more power than the sword. The sister of the native's wife will prove highly helpful in every matter. If a Moon is placed in the 1st house, overseas journey will be advantageous. Saturn in the 3rd house will make the wife's family very rich.

Remedies

1. Avoid any business in partnership.
2. Avoid speculation.
3. Do not keep relationship with sister in law of spoilt character.

Mercury in 8th House

Mercury gives very bad results in 8th house, but if it is placed along with a male planet it will give good effects of the associated planet. The native lives a hard life, victimized by diseases and during the age 32-34 his income goes down by half. It is more harmful if some planet is placed in the 2nd house. If Rahu is also placed in the same house the native may have to go to jail, may have to be hospitalized or may have to wander from place to place. Bad results accrue if mars are also placed therein. Mercury here causes disfavor from the government and diseases like blood disorder, eye problem, tooth and vein troubles, as well as big loss in business.

Remedies

1. Get an earthen pot filled with honey and bury it in the cremation ground or deserted area.
2. Place milk or rain water in a container on the roof of the house.
3. Put a ring in the nose of your daughter.

Mercury in 9th House

Mercury provides very bad results in the 9th house also, because this house belongs to Jupiter and Mercury remains inimical to it. It causes continuous mental restlessness and defamation of various types. If moon, Ketu and Jupiter are placed in 1, 3, 6, 7, 9 and 11th houses, mercury does not give very advantageous results. Remedies

1. Avoid the use of green color.
2. Get your nose pricked.
3. Offer mushroom filled in an earthen pot to a religious place.
4. Do not accept any tabeez from any sadhoo or faqir.

Mercury in 10th House

Mercury in the 10th house provides favor from the government. Gives good sources of livelihood. he manages to get his work done in every way. The business of such a native flourishes in a shermukhi house, but residency in such a house gives very bad result and can be disastrous.

Remedies

1. Consumption of eggs, meat and liquor are strictly prohibited.
2. Offer rice and milk in religious places.

Mercury in 11th House

Mercury in this house gives bad results, because of enmity to Jupiter. At the age of 34 the native undertakes works of extreme foolishness. Here mercury causes loss of wealth, loss of mental peace and loss of reputation. Even hard work is not awarded. However the children of native will be well educated and get married in very rich and noble families.

Remedies

1. Wear copper coin in neck in a white thread or silver chain.
2. Do not keep a widowed sister or father's sister in your house.

3. Avoid green color and emerald.
4. Do not accept any Tabeez from a sadhoo or faqir.

Mercury in 12th House

Mercury here destroys night's sleep of the native and causes troubles of many sorts. He loses peace of mind and very often suffers from headache. He has a long life but suffers from mercury, although, however, if mercury is accompanied by Saturn in this house very good results follow. Saturn along with sun and Mercury in 12th house also give good result. Daughters, sisters, father's sister and niece will be unhappy as long as they are living in the native's house. Such persons are generally self-praising and of irritable nature. If something right or wrong goes into his mind, he will ensure to stick to it in every manner. If such a native is fond of taking liquor he will be of pretentious nature. Speculation in business will prove harmful. Marriage in the 25th year will prove harmful for the native's wife and father.

Remedies

1. Throwing new empty pitcher in a river.
2. Putting on a ring of stainless steel.
3. Putting kesar tilak on face, head and visiting religious places of worship.
4. Taking advice of another person before starting any new or important work.

GEMS FOR MERCURY

EMERALD

GREEN

Chapter Nine

KETU

Effects and Remedies

Ketu, according to the author of Lal Kitab, represents son, grandson, ear, spine etc. 6th house is considered to be its own strong house.' It gives its exalted effect when in 5th, 9th or 12th house and its debilitated effect in 6th and 8th house.

Dawn is its time and it represents Sunday. Ketu represents the opposite node of Ketu, in the tail of the serpent. Its colours are black and white. Venus and Rahu are its friends, whereas Moon and Mars are its enemies. Forty two years is the age of Ketu. Ketu is also considered to be the bed. So the bed given by in-laws after marriage is considered to be auspicious for the birth of a son and as long as that bed is in the house, the effect of Ketu can never be inauspicious.

GENER REMEDIES FOR PLANET KETU IN BRIEF

1. Prepare Sour Rice, any rice dish which is extremely sour.
2. Stand under a banyan tree.
3. Place the dish on a dry Butea monosperma leaf.
4. Hold it in your hand and recite Ketu mantra/sloka.

SPECIAL REMEDIES FOR PLANET KETU IN DETAIL

Ketu in 1st House

If Ketu is auspicious or benefic in this house, the native will be laborious, rich and happy, but will always be concerned and troubled because of his progeny. He may fear frequent transfers or travels, but ultimately it would always be postponed.

Whenever Ketu comes in 1st house in Varsha Kundli there may be birth of a son or nephew. There may also be a long journey. The native with Ketu in 1st house will always be beneficial for his father and/or guru and causes exaltation of Sun.

If Ketu in 1st house is malefic, the native would suffer from headache. His wife would have health problems and would have worries concerning kids. If 2nd and 7th houses are empty then Mercury and Venus would also give bad results. There would be travels, transfers with no gain. If Saturn is malefic it would destroy father and guru.

If Sun is in 7th or 8th house then after the birth of a grandson the health would suffer. No alms should be given in morning and evening.

Remedies

1. Feed jaggery (gur) to monkeys.
2. Apply saffron as Tilak.
3. If offspring is troubled then donate a black and white blanket to temple.

Ketu in 2nd House

2nd house is affected by Moon, which is an enemy of Ketu. If Ketu in 2nd house is benefic then one gets paternal property. One has to travel a lot and his travels are fruitful. Venus gives good results, irrespective of its position. Moon would give bad results. If Sun is in 12th house then one starts earning his livelihood after twenty four years and is happy. If Jupiter is exalted along with Ketu in 2nd house, then income would be in lacs of rupees. If Ketu in 2nd house is malefic, then one has to travel to dry areas. One cannot rest at one place and would be wandering from place to place. Income may be good, but so would be the expenditure. Thus net gain would be negligible. If there is Moon or Mars in 8th house then native's life would be short and he would have serious problem at the age of sixteen or twenty years. If 8th house is empty then Ketu would give malefic results.

Remedies

1. Apply turmeric or saffron as tilak.
2. One should not be of loose character.
3. If one religiously visits temples and bows his head there then Ketu in 2nd house would give good results.

Ketu in 3rd House

3rd house is affected by Mercury and Mars, both enemies of Ketu. Number 3 would have an important role in the life of the native. If Ketu in 3rd house is benefic then his children would be good. The native would be god fearing and a gentleman. If Ketu is in 3rd house and Mars is in 12th then the native has a son before 24th year of age. The son would be good for wealth and longevity of the native. The native with Ketu in 3rd house usually gets a job, which entails long travels.

If Ketu in 3rd house is malefic then native loses money in litigation. He gets separated from his wife/sisters-in-law. If such a native lives in a house with its main gate facing south, he will have serious problems regarding children. Such a native cannot say no to anything and so will always have worries. He will have troubles from his brothers and will have to travel uselessly.

Remedies

1. Use saffron as tilak.
2. Wear gold.
3. Offer jaggery, rice in flowing water.

Ketu in 4th house

4th house belongs to Moon, which is an enemy of Ketu. If Ketu is benefic in 4th house then the native is god fearing and lucky for his father and guru. Son is born to such a native only after getting the blessings of one's guru. The son born lives long. Such a native leaves all his decisions to God. If moon is in 3rd or 4th house the result is benefic. Such a native is a good adviser and will never have shortage of money. If Ketu is malefic in this house then the native is unhealthy, his mother is troubled, and there is loss of happiness. One may suffer from diabetes. A son is born after thirty six years of age. Such a native has more daughters than sons.

Remedies

1. Keep a dog.
2. Wear silver for peace of mind.
3. Offer yellow things in flowing water.

Ketu in 5th House

5th house belongs to Sun. It is also affected by Jupiter. If Jupiter, Sun or Moon is in 4th, 6th or 12th house then one's financial condition will be excellent and the native will have five sons. Ketu becomes benefic by itself after twenty four years of age. If Ketu in 5th house is malefic then the native suffers from asthma. Ketu gives malefic results till five years of age. Sons will not survive. Livelihood starts after twenty four years of age. The native is unlucky for one's sons.

Remedies

1. Donate milk and sugar.
2. The remedies of Jupiter would be useful.

Ketu in 6th House

6th house belongs to Mercury. Ketu in 6th house is considered debilitated. This is strong house of Ketu. Here again the effect of Ketu depends upon the nature of Jupiter. It gives good result regarding son. The native is a good adviser.

If Jupiter is benefic then the native has a long life and his mother is happy and the life is peaceful. If any two of the male planets via Sun, Jupiter, Mars are in good position then Ketu is benefic.

If Ketu is malefic in 6th house then maternal uncle suffers. The native has to suffer due to useless travels. People turn into enemies without any reason. The native suffers from skin diseases. If Moon is in 2nd house then mother suffers and even the native's old age is troubled.

Remedies

1. Wear golden ring in the finger of left hand.
2. Drink milk with saffron and wear gold in the ear.
3. Heat up a rod of gold and then dip it in milk. Then drink it. It would restore mental peace, increase longevity and is good for sons.
4. Keep a dog.

Ketu in 7th House

7th house belongs to Mercury and Venus. If Ketu in 7th house is benefic then the native gets the wealth of forty years in twenty four years of age. The wealth increases in proportion to the children one has. The native's enemies are frightened of the native. If one has the help of Mercury, Jupiter or Venus then the native is never disappointed.

If Ketu in 7th house is malefic then the native is usually ill, makes false promises and is troubled by enemies till thirty four years of age. If there are more than one planet in Lagna then ones children are destroyed. If one abuses then the native is destroyed. If Ketu is with Mercury then after thirty four years of age the native's enemies are destroyed by themselves.

Remedies

1. Never make a false promise, be proud, or abusive.
2. Use saffron as Tilak.
3. In case of serious trouble use the remedies of Jupiter.

Ketu in 8th house

8th house belongs to Mars, which is an enemy of Ketu. If Ketu in 8th house is benefic then the native begets a son at thirty four years of age, or after the marriage of one's sister or daughter. If Jupiter or Mars are not in 6th and 12th house then Ketu does not give malefic results. Similar effect is there when

Moon is in 2nd house. If Ketu in 8th house is malefic then the native's wife has ill health. son will not be born, or may die. The native may suffer from diabetes or urinary problem. If Saturn or Mars are in 7th then the native is unlucky. In case of malefic Ketu in 8th house the native's character determines the health of his wife. After twenty six years of age the family life suffers.

Remedies

1. Keep a dog.
2. Donate a black and white blanket in any temple.
3. Worship lord Ganesh.
4. Wear gold in the ear.
5. Use saffron as tilak.

Ketu in 9th House

9th house belongs to Jupiter, which favors Ketu. Ketu in 9th house is considered to be exalted. Such a native is obedient and lucky. It increases ones wealth. If Ketu is benefic then one earns wealth through one's own labor. There will be progress but no transfer. If one keeps gold brick in his house then wealth comes. The son of such a native is able to guess the future. One spends a big part of his life in foreign land. One has at least three sons and if 2nd house is auspicious then Ketu gives excellent results. If Moon is auspicious then the native helps his mother's family. If Ketu in 9th house is malefic then the native suffers from urinary problems, pain in back, and problem in legs. The native's sons keep on dying.

Remedies

1. Keep a dog.

1. Establish a rectangular piece of gold anywhere in the house.
2. Wear gold in the ear.
3. Respect elders, especially father-in-law.

Ketu in 10th house.

10th house belongs to Saturn. The effect of Ketu here depends upon the nature of Saturn. If Ketu is benefic here then the native is lucky, concerned about himself and opportunist. His father dies early. If Saturn is in 6th then one is a famous player. If one keeps on forgiving his brothers for their misdeeds the native will go on progressing. If the character of native is good then he earns a lot of wealth. If Ketu in 10th house is malefic then one suffers from urinary and ear problems. The native has pain in bones. The domestic life is full of worries and troubled if Saturn is in 4th house. Three sons would die.

Remedies

1. Keep silver pot full of honey in the house.
2. Keep a dog, especially after forty eight years of age.
3. Avoid adultery.
4. Use the remedies of Moon and Jupiter.

Ketu in 11th House

Here Ketu is considered very good. It gives wealth. This house is affected by Jupiter and Saturn. If Ketu is benefic here and Saturn is in 3rd house, it gives enormous wealth. The wealth earned by the native is more than his paternal wealth, but one tends to worry about his future. If Mercury is in 3rd it leads to Raj Yoga. If Ketu is malefic here then the native has problem in his abdomen. The more he worries about future, more troubled he is. Grandmother or mother of the native suffers, if Saturn is also malefic. Then there would be no benefit from son or house.

Remedies

1. Keep black dog.
2. Wear an onyx or emerald.

Ketu in 12th House

Here Ketu is considered to be exalted. The native is wealthy, achieves a big position and spends on good works. If Rahu is in 6th house, along with Mercury, then the effect is even better. One has all the benefits and luxuries of life. If Ketu in 12th house is malefic then one buys land from an issueless person and the native becomes issueless himself. If one kills dogs Ketu gives malefic results. If 2nd house has Moon, Venus or Mars, Ketu gives malefic results.

Remedies

1. Worship Lord Ganesh.
2. Do not have a loose character.
3. Keep a dog.
4. Saunf and khand under the pillow for good night's sleep.

GEMS FOR KETU

CAT'S EYE OFF WHITE

Chapter Ten

VENUS

Effects and Remedies

As a feminine planet, Venus has been regarded as the goddess of love, marriage, beauty and all worldly comforts. Venus represents that power of love which leads to the merger of two individual selves into one and rules the gentle and refined attributes of human life.

As a preceptor of demons, Venus stands for the husband in the horoscope of a female and represents the wife in the horoscope of a male. Venus offers good results if placed alone in the birth chart. the 2nd and 7th houses are owned by Venus who gets exalted in the 12th house. Saturn, Mercury and Ketu are friends of Venus, whereas Sun, Moon and Rahu act as enemies.

Venus offers very good results if posited in the 2nd, 3rd, 4th, 7th and 12th houses, but the 1st, 6th and 9th houses are considered bad for Venus. Accordingly, Venus offers very good results in the houses of Mercury, Saturn and Ketu, whereas evil effects will follow if posited in the houses of Sun, Rahu and Moon. When Rahu aspects Venus or vice versa, or when both are placed together in a house, the good results of Venus will be nullified and the native will get deprived of money, wealth and family comforts altogether. The eyes of the native's, mother will become severely defective if Moon and Venus are placed just opposite to each other.

Afflicted Venus causes trouble in the eyes, diseases of the ovaries, gout, anemia and other complications due to over indulgence in amusements and sex, including gonorrhea and syphilis. An afflicted Venus may cause vehicular accidents, faithlessness in love and marriage and will deprive the native of the comforts of vehicles, conveyance etc.

GENERAL REMEDIES FOR PLANET VENUS IN BRIEF

Venus: Offer Ghee rice (clarified butter) in a silver dish to any Goddess on Friday and distribute it to people or family before you consume. If you mess this process, you will get even fatter (just so you know). If you don't have silver dish or pure ghee don't try this.

SPECIAL REMEDIES FOR PLANET VENUS IN DETAIL

Venus in 1st House

Venus in 1st house makes the native highly handsome, long lived, sweet tongued and popular among the opposite sex. Wife of the native remains ill. Religion, caste or creed is never a bar for having sexual relations with anyone. Such a native is generally highly romantic by nature and longs for love and sex with other women. He gets married before he starts earning his living. Such a native becomes a leader of persons of his age group, but leadership of the family members causes several family troubles. Such a native earns great profits through the trade of clothes. Such a native is generally deprived of interest in religious pursuits. When Venus comes in 7th house in Varsha phal, it causes chronic fever and blood cough.

Remedies

1. Do not marry at the age of 25 years.
2. Always act according to the advice of others.
3. Serving a black cow.
4. Avoid sex during day time.
5. Take bath with curd.
6. Intake of cow's urine is very useful.

Venus in 2nd House

Doing bad or evil towards others would prove harmful to the native. Money, wealth and property would continue to grow up to sixty years. Shermukhi house (wider at the front than the rear portion) would prove disastrous for the native. Business or trade associated with gold and jewelry will be extremely harmful. Business associated with earthen goods, agriculture and animal will prove highly beneficial. Venus in 2nd second house in a female horoscope renders the native barren or infertile and in a male's horoscope makes the wife incapable of producing a son.

Remedies

1. For getting a son, intake of things associated with mars like honey, Saunf or deshi Khand will be highly effective.
2. Feed two kgs of potatoes colored by yellow turmeric to cows.
3. Offer two kgs. Cow's ghee in a temple.
4. Avoid adultery.

Venus in 3rd House

Here Venus blesses the native with a charming personality and every woman would get attracted to him. He is generally loved by all.

If the native gets involved with other women he will have to live in subservience to his wife, otherwise his wife will always be dominated by him, though she may be dominating everyone else coming into contact with her. She would be courageous, supportive and helpful to the native like second bullock of the cart. He will be saved from deceit, theft and harm from others. Contacts with other women would prove harmful and affect the longevity adversely. If planets placed in 9th and 11th houses are inimical to Venus, highly adverse results will follow. He will have many daughters.

Remedies

1. Respect your wife and never insult her.
2. Avoid flirting with other women.

Venus in 4th House

Venus in 4th house strongly establishes the possibility of two wives and makes the native rich, too, If Jupiter is posited in 10th house and Venus is placed in 4th, the native will face adverse results from all sides if he tries to be religious.

Venus in 4th house destroys the possibility of a son to the native if he covers a well by a roof and constructs a room or house over it. The business associated with mercury will also prove harmful. Saturn will give disastrous effects if the native consumes liquor. The business or trade associated with mars will prove advantageous to such a native. Venus in 4th and Jupiter in Ist house will create frequent quarrels with the mother-in-law.

Remedies

1. Change the name of your wife and remarry her formally.
2. Throwing rice, silver and milk in the running water or feeding Kheer or milk to mother like women will ward off the quarrels between mother-in-law and daughter-in-law.
3. Keep the roof of the house clean and well-maintained for the health of your wife.
4. Drop things of Jupiter, like gram, pulses and Kesar, in the river.

Venus in 5th house

5th house is the Solid house of the sun, where Venus will get burnt with the heat of the Sun. Consequently the native is a flirt and amorous by nature. he will face big misfortunes in life. However, if the native maintains a good character he will steer through the hardships of life and obtain great riches and promotions in service after five years of his marriage. Such a native is generally learned and destroyer of enemies.

Remedies

1. One should not marry against the wishes of his parents.
2. Serving cows and mother like women.
3. Avoid relationship will other women.
4. Native's wife should wash her private parts with curd or milk.

Venus in 6th House

This house belongs to mercury and Ketu, who are inimical to each other, but Venus is friendly to both. Venus stands, debilitated in this house. However, if the native keeps the opposite sex happy and provides her with all the comforts, his money and wealth will continue to grow. The wife of the native should not get dressed like a male and should not get her hair cut like a male, otherwise poverty will crop up. Such a native must marry a person who has got a brother or brothers. Further, the native should not leave any work in the midway, i.e., before completion.

Remedies

1. Ensure that your wife puts gold clips in her hair.
2. Your spouse must not remain barefooted.
3. The private parts should be washed with red medicine.

Venus in 7th House

This house belongs to Venus, so Venus gives very good results if it is placed in this house. The planet of 1st house offers the effects of 7th house in such a manner as if it is placed in 7th house itself. If a planet inimical to Venus is placed in Ist house e.g. Rahu, the wife and the household affairs of the native will be adversely affected. The native spends his money largely on women. The native should take up the trade or business which is associated will marriage ceremony, like tent house and beauty parlor. Association with one eyed and black woman will prove useful.

Remedies

1. Domestication of white cows prohibited.
2. Serving red cows.
3. Donate Jawar equal to the weight of your spouse to a temple.
4. Throwing blue flowers in a dirty canal for 43 days.

Venus in 8th House

No planet is considered benefic in this house Even Venus in this house becomes rotten and poisonous. The wife of such a native becomes highly irritable and short tempered. Evil utterances from her mouth will certainly prove to be true. The native will be suffering from the feeling of self-pity. Taking guarantee or surety for someone will prove disastrous. If there is no planet in 2nd house, do not marry before 25 years of age, otherwise the wife will certainly die.

Remedies

1. The native should not accept daan.
2. Bowing head in the place of worship and temples.
3. Copper coin or blue flower to be thrown in gutter or dirty Nullah continuously for ten days.
4. Wash your private parts with curd.

Venus in 9th House

Venus in this house does not offer good results. The native may have riches, but he will get his bread only after hard labor. His efforts are not properly rewarded. There will be dearth of male members, money, wealth and property. If Venus is accompanied by Mercury or any malefic planet the native will be a victim of intoxication and disease from seventeen years of age.

Remedies

1. In the foundation of the house silver and honey should be buried.
2. Silver bangles to be worn after putting some red color on them.
3. Bury a silver piece under a Neem tree for 43 days.

Venus in 10th House

Venus in this house makes native greedy, suspicious and interested in handicraft. The native would act under the control and guidance of his spouse. as long as the spouse is with the native all sorts of troubles will remain warded off. If in a motor car no accident will take place or even if it takes place the native cannot be harmed in any manner. The business and things associated with Saturn will prove advantageous.

Remedies

1. Washing private parts with curd.
2. Western wall of the house should be of mud.
3. Abstinence from wine and non-vegetarian food.
4. At the time of illness, the native should donate a black cow.

Venus in 11th House

Venus in this house is influenced by Saturn and Jupiter, because this house belongs to Jupiter and Saturn. This house is aspected by 3rd house which is influenced by Mars and Mercury. Native's wife, through her brothers, will prove very beneficial.

Remedies

1. Remedies of Mercury will be useful.
2. Oil to be given on Saturday.
3. The native usually suffers from low sperm count in his semen. Native should drink milk in which hot piece of gold has been dipped.

Venus in 12th House

Exalted Venus gives very beneficial results in this house. The native will have a wife, who will act as a shield in the time of trouble. Taking help from women will prove highly advantageous for the native, who receives all favors from the government.

Venus being inimical to Jupiter causes health problems to the wife. Mercury in 2nd or 6th houses makes the native diseased, but bestows literary and poetic talent to the native. such a native gains high spiritual powers at the age of 59 and generally lives up to about 96 years.

Remedies

1. Blue flowers to be buried by the wife at the time of sunset, for good health.

2. The wife will act as a defense wall for the husband, if she gives things in charity to people.
3. Domesticating and giving cows in charity.
4. Offer love, respect and honor to your wife.

GEM FOR VENUS

DIAMOND

COLORLESS

Chapter Eleven

PLANETARY GEMSTONES

The ancient kings, queens, and royal persons of India always had an astrologer in their court.

In addition to reading charts and making predictions, the astrologer would also recommend the proper gemstones, which were then worn on the crowns, and as rings and pendants.

The gemstones are related to the various planets, and are said to bring the planetary energies into the physiology, thus helping with health, courage, wisdom, compassion, creativity, and even longevity of life.

It is important, however, to only wear the gemstones of the favorable planets in your chart, and to avoid wearing the gemstones of the planets that can cause adverse effects.

Find out which gemstones are most beneficial for your birth chart.

Astrological Gemstones and
Corresponding
Planets

Ruling Planet Sign Ruled Primary Gem

1. Secondary Gem
2. (Uparatna)
3. 3rd Choice
4. 4th Choice
5. Sun Leo Ruby (Heatedor Unheated)
6. Red Spinel Rhodolite Rubellite

7. Moon
8. Cancer
9. Natural Pearl
10. Tissue Nucleated Pearl
11. South Sea Pearl
12. Moonstone

13. Mars
14. Aries, Scorpio
15. Red Coral
16. Carnelian-

17. Mercury
18. Gemini, Virgo
19. Emerald
20. Green Tourmaline
21. Peridot

22. Jupiter
23. Sagittarius, Pisces
24. Yellow Sapphire
25. Yellow Topaz Citrine

26. Venus
27. Taurus, Libra
28. Diamond
29. White Sapphire
30. Phenakite White Zircon

31. Saturn
32. Capricorn, Aquarius
33. Blue Sapphire
34. Blue Spinel
35. Amethyst

Rahu

36. Hessonite (Gomed)
37. Spessartite

38. Ketu
39. Chrysoberyl Cat's Eye

Chapter Twelve

BRIEF DISCRIPTION OF YOUR NUMBERS
AND
BRIEF REMEDIES OF YOUR NUMBERS

GEMS AND STONES FOR ALL NUMBERS

Gem Stone for No. 1

Number 1—Initiative, independence, forcefulness (a masculine number).

The best suited stone or gem according to numerology for number one is Ruby. It enhances your fortune or your luck powerfully. Alternately you can also use yellow sapphire and Topaz. These would help improve your health and give you success in your actions, deeds and in your life.

We could find that these gems, helps in promoting healthy growth in our young sons and daughters. As an grown up person, you could wear Ruby or yellow sapphire. Both are fine for you. You have to wear it in your right hand in ring finger made in gold ring.

Gem Stone for No. 2

Number 2—Tact, diplomacy, attention to details (a feminine number).

The best suited stone or gem according to numerology for number two is Pearl. It enhances your fortune or your luck abundantly. Alternately you can also use Jade, Moon stone, and Tiger's Eye. These would help improve your health and give you success in your actions, deeds in your life.

All are fine for you. You have to wear it in your right hand in smallest finger made in silver ring. Jade has a particular medical use. It relieves your stomach disorders. The Tigers Eye is good for your children.

Gems for No. 3

Number 3—Self-expression, ambition, spirituality, luck, easy success.

The best suited stone or gem according to numerology for number three is Amethyst. Amethyst is of a violet color. There are many benefits. It enhances your luck abundantly. Alternately known for its anti-drunkenness properties, it greatly powers you up in your decisions.

It prevents you forever from becoming over intoxicated. These would help improve your health and give you success in your actions, deeds in your life. You can also use yellow sapphire with a golden hue. It is also highly favorable for you. It enhances your luck and worldly success. You must were your gem in your left hand, in your ring finger, studding it over gold.

Gems for no 4

Number 4—Labor, material, routine work—little paid compensation, unlucky.

The best suited stone or gem according to numerology for number Four is Garnet.. There are many benefits. It enhances your luck abundantly. The next choice is blue sapphire. Select it with the blue light color. Alternatively opal can also be used.

Gems for No. 5

Number 5—Inventive genius, imagination, charm, restlessness, adventurous.

The best suited stone or gem according to numerology for number Five is, Diamond. It should be highly of good quality and have the specification and be genuinely pure. It should be seen that it need to shine with the glow of the light. Zircon can be used as an alternate gem.

Gems for No. 6

Number 6—Tenacity, conscientiousness, achievement by working with others, domestic.

The best suited stone or gem according to numerology for number six is Emerald. Circular or opal size structure should be taken. It powers mental strength, self-confidence, and immense happiness. It should be a flawless piece having some luster.

Gems for No.7

Number 7—Mysticism, isolation, poets and dreamers; misunderstood by co-workers or companions.

The best suited stone or gem according to numerology for number seven is Cat's Eye. There are many benefits. It enhances your fortune and makes you very strong.

Gems for Number 8

Number 8—Reason, judgment, financial success, organization.

The best suited stone or gem according to numerology for number eight is Blue Sapphire. It can be tested, put a piece of blue sapphire in a glass of milk and if the there is a bluish layer than it is a good gem to be worn. High quality Sapphire showers good luck.

Gems for number 9

Number 9—Sympathy, generosity, dramatic, artistic talent (higher octave—teacher, master).

The best suited stone or gem according to numerology for number nine is Coral. It comes from the deep seas from the coral rocks, created by coral making insects. It removes blood related diseases and showers immense Luck. It gives you victory over your enemies. It bestows health and riches.

Chapter Thirteen

MANTRAS AND REMEDIES FOR THE NINE PLANETS

There several mantras and remedies for the planets prescribed in the various scriptures. We are giving bellow the most effective ones in our experience.

Surya

For Surya or Sun related troubles and during the dasa or antardasa of sun:

BRIEF REMEDIES FOR PLANET SUN

1. Worship the ruling deity Lord Shiva
    Recite Aditya Hridaya stotra daily or
2. Gayatri Mantra daily.
3. Japa of Sun's moola mantra: "Om hram hreem hroum sah suryaya namah", 6000 times in 40 days.

Recite the soorya stotra:
4. Java kusuma sankasam kashyapeyam mahadutimTamorim Sarva paapghnam pranatosmi Divakaram
5. Charity: Donate wheat, or sugar candy on sunday.
5. Fasting day: Sundays.
6. Pooja: Rudrabhishek.
7. Rudraksha: Wear Ekamukhi or 12 mukhi Rudraksha

BRIEF REMEDIES FOR PLANET MOON

For Moon related problems and during the dasa or antardasa of Moon:

1. Worship the ruling deity Gouri.

2. Recite Annapoorna stotram.
3. Japa of Moon's moola mantra:
   Om shram sreem shraum sah chandraya namah, 10000 times in 40 days.

Recite the Chandra stotra:

4. Dadhi Shankha tushaarabham ksheero darnava ambhavamNamaami shashinam somam shambhor mukuta bhushanam
5. Charity: Donate cow's milk or rice on Monday.
6. Fasting: On Mondays.
7. Pooja: Devi pooja.
8. Rudraksha: Wear 2 mukhi Rudraksha.

BRIEF REMEDIES FOR PLANET MARS

Mangal

For Mangal or Mars related problems and during the dasa or antardasa of Mars:

1. Worship the ruling deities Kartikeya and Shiva.
2. The Kartikeya mantra is "Om Saravanabhavaya Namah"
3. The Shiva mantra is "Om Namah Shivaya" Recite Kartikeya or Shiva stotra.

1. Japa of the Mars mantra: Om kram kreem kroum sah bhaumaya namah, 7000 times in 40 days.

Recite the Mangala stotra:

4. Dharani garbha sambhutam vidyut kanti samaprabhamKumaram shakti hastam tam mangalam pranamamyaham.
5. Charity: Donate Masoor dal(red lentils) on tuesday.
6. Fasting: On Tuesdays.
7. Pooja: Kartikeya pooja or Rudrabhishekha.
8. Rudraksha: Wear a 3 mukhi Rudraksha.

Mars is also the remover of debts and the giver of wealth. The following is a highly recommended stotra of Mars for this purpose.

Angarakoyamaschaiva sarvarogaapahaarakah

Nrishtekargaacha hartaacha sarvadevascha poojitah.

Lohito Lohitaakshascha samagaanaKripaakarah

Dharmatmajah Kujobhoumou bhumido bhuminam

Rakta maalyambaradharam shulashakti gadaadharah

Charbhujo yeshagato varadamcha dharaasutah

Mangalo bhumiputrascha runahartaa dhanapradah Sthiraasano mahaakaayo sarvakaama phalapradam

BRIEF REMEDIES FOR PLANET MERCURY

For Budha or Mercury related problems and during his dasa and antardasa:

1. Worship Lord Vishnu.
2. Recite Vishnu sahasranama stotra.
3. Japa of the Budha beeja mantra:
   Om bram breem broum sah budhaya namah, 17000 times in 40 days.

Recite the Budha stotra:
4. Priyangu Kalika Shyaamam Roopena Pratimam Budham Soumyam Soumya gunopetam tam Budham Pranamamyaham.
5. Charity: Donate Udad dal on Wednesday.
6. Fasting: On Wednesdays.
7. Pooja: Vishnu pooja.
8. Wear a 10 mukhi Rudraksha.

BRIEF REMEDIES FOR PLANET JUPITER

For Guru or Jupiter related problems and during the dasa or antardasa of Guru:

1. Worship Lord Shiva.

Recite Shri Rudram.
2. Japa of the Guru beeja mantra: Om jhram jhreem jroum sah gurave namah, 16000 times in 40 days.

Recite the Guru stotra:
> Devanam cha rishinam cha Gurum kaanchan SannibhaamBuddhi bhutam Trilokesham tam namaami Brihaspatim.
3. Donate: Saffron or turmeric or sugar on Thursdayon.
4. Fasting: On Thrusdays.
5. Pooja: Rudrabhishekam.
6. Wear a 5 mukhi rudraksha.

BRIEF REMEDIES FOR PLANET VENUS

For Shukra or Venus related problems and during the dasa or antardasa of Venus:

1. Worship Devi.
   Recite Shree Sooktam or Devi stuti or Durga chalisa.
2. Japa of Shukra beeja mantra: Om dram dreem droum sah shukraya namah, 20000 times in 40 days.

Recite the Shukra stotra:
> Hima kunda mrinalaabham daityanam paramam gurumSarv shastra pravaktaram bhargavem pranamamyaham
3. Donate clothes or dairy cream or curd to a lady on Friday.
4. Fasting: On Fridays.
5. Pooja: Devi pooja.
6. Wear a 9 mukhi Rudraksha.

BRIEF REMEDIES FOR PLANET SATURN

For Shani or Saturn related problems and during the dasa or antardasa of Shani:

1. Worship Lord Hanuman.
2. Recite Hanuman chalisa or any other Hanuman stotra.
3. Japa of Shani mantra: Om pram preem proum sah shanaischaraya namah, 19000 times in 40 days.
4. Recite the Shani stotra:
5. Nelanjan samabhasam ravi putram yamagrajamChaaya martand sambhutam tam namami shanaischaram
6. Donate a buffalo or black til (sesame seeds) on Saturday.
7. Fasting on Saturdays.
8. Puja: Hanuman puja
9. Wear a 14 mukhi Rudraksha.

For all Saturn related troubles Dasharatha Shani Stotra of is an excellent remedy.

BRIEF REMEDIES FOR PLANET RAHU

DRAGON'S HEAD

For Rahu related problems and during the dasa or antardasa of Rahu:

1. Worship Bhairava or lord Shiva.
   Recite the Kalabhairav asthakam.
2. Japa of the rahu beeja mantra:
   Om bhram bhreem bhroum sah rahave namah, 18000 times in 40 days.

Recite the Rahu stotra:
   Ardha Kaayam maha veryam chandraditya vimardhanamSimhika garbha sambhutam tam rahum pranamamyaham.
3. Donate: Udad dal or coconut on Saturday.
4. Fasting on Saturdays.

5. Pooja: Bhairav or Shiva or Chandi pooja.
6. Wear An 8 mukhi Rudraksha.
7. One of the best remedies for rahu is reciting the first chapter of Durga Saptasati.

BRIEF REMEDIES FOR PLANET KETU

DRAGON'S TAIL

For Ketu related problems and during the dasa or antardasa of Ketu:

1. Worship Lord Ganesha.
   Recite Ganesha Dwadasanama Stotra.
2. Japa of the Ketu beeja mantra: Om shram shreem shroum sah ketave namah, 7000 times in 40 days.

Recite the Ketu stotra:
Palasha pushpa sankaasham taraka graha mastakamRoudram roudratmakam ghoram tam ketum Pranamamyaham.

1. Donate: A black cow or black mustard seeds on thursday.
2. Fasting: On Thursdays.
3. Pooja: Ganesh pooja.
4. Wear a 9 mukhi rudraksha
5. A very good remedy for Ketu is the reciting of Shiva Panchakshari Stotra.

Chapter Fourteen

MANTRAS

Sun:

Om Bhaskaraya Vidmahe Mahadyutikaraya Dhimahi Tanno Aditya Prachodayat

Moon:

Om Ksheeraputraya Vidmahe Amruta-tatvaya Dhimahi Tanno Chandra Prachodayat

Mars:

Om Angarakaya Vidmahe Sakti Hastaya Dhimahi Tanno Bhaumah Prachodayat

Saturn:

Om Neelanjanaya Vidmahe Chhayamartandaya Dhimahi TannoShani PrachodayatPlanetary

Chapter Fifteen

The astrological remedies can broadly be broken up in three parts:

Mantra—

It is the recitation of a particular sound repeatedly to overcome the problems set forth by the planet which responds to that particular sound. The basis of mind in its objective and structural aspect is the power inherent in different combinations of sounds. How consciousness differentiates into different states of mind is an interesting question and is impossible to know in the real sense until we can raise our consciousness to the level where this differentiation takes place and the manner in which it is brought about. Each root word generates a sound that activates a different center in the human body that correlates to the particular planet.

Tantra—

At times when the Mantra does not work because of difficult malefic position of planets in a horoscope in that case Tantric sound patterns work like surgery and clears most of the hurdles.

Yantra—

This is a Mystic diagram often put up as a plaque. Some Yantra are a part of Tantra practice since Yantra is one of the cardinal principles of Tantra. This practise is followed when a particular remedy has to be practised over a long period of time and the querist is unable to perform other remedial measures due to ill-health, lack of time or distance.

Besides this there are the common remedies in form of Gems & Metals in combination worn to help tide over malefic effects of planets.

But in some severe cases it has been noticed that the Malefic Effects of bad planetary combinations are such to push a person into abnormal mental stress, giving life threatening ailments or push a person to the brink of bankruptcy. Also in case of problematic birth stars a child is destined to lead a hollow life unless propriatory measures are taken to rectify the same (Birth in Moola Nakshatra etc).

Even marriages where the matching was not adhered to attract a lot of problem which can partially be solved with the help of remedies.

Chapter Sixteen

There are many Planets in our System on which all calculations are based. Each planet rules a particular sign and has individual characteristic, vibration, trait that influences the person born under it. Each planet is given a number. The Nine Planets, with Corresponding Numbers and their Zodiac signs are:

The sun and the moon are the only two planets having 'double numbers'. The sun and Uranus are interrelated and so is the moon and Neptune. There is a strong attraction between numbers 1-4 and 2-7 and these four numbers are compatible with each other.

Numbers 7 and 4 were allotted to the moon and the sun until Neptune and Uranus were discovered. Presently, number 4 is the number of planet Uranus or Rahu

PLANET	RULES NUMBER	ZODIAC SIGNs
Mars	9	Aries
Venus	6	Taurus
Mercury	5	Gemini
Moon	2, 7	Cancer
Sun	1, 4	Leo
Mercury	5	Virgo
Venus	6	Libra
Mars	9	Scorpio
Jupiter	3	Sagittarius
Saturn	8	Capricorn Aquarius
Jupiter	3	Pisces

. . . . THE . . . . END . . . .

Our First Two Publications
Are On Sale

1. "'MICROSCOPY OF ASTROLOGY'"
2. "'MICROSCOPY OF NUMEROLOGY'"

ORDERS FOR BOOKS CAN BE PLACED AT:

orders.india@partridgepublishing.com
channelsales@authorsolutions.com

AND AT OUR CONTACT ADDRESS:

PLEASE SEND YOUR QUERIES TO:

BALDEV BHATIA
CONSULTANT-NUMEROLOGY-ASTROLOGY
C-63, FIRST FLOOR
MALVIYA NAGAR
NEW DELHI-110017
INDIA

TEL NO 919810075249
TEL NO 91 11 26686856
TEL NO 91 7503280786
TEL NO 91 7702735880

MAIL US AT:

baldevbhatia@yahoo.com

OUR MOST SOUGHT WEB SITES:

HTTP://WWW.ASTROLOGYBB.COM
HTTP://WWW.BBASTROLOGY.COM
HTTP://WWW.BALDEVBHATIA.COM
HTTP://WWW.BALDEVBHATIA.US
HTTP://WWW.BALDEVBHATIA.ORG
HTTP://WWW.BALDEVBHATIA.INFO
HTTP://WWW.BALDEVBHATIA.NET
HTTP://WWW.BALDEVBHATIA.BIZ
HTTP://WWW.BALDEVBHATIA.IN
HTTP://WWW.MICROSCOPYOFASTROLOGY.COM

Special Note

FROM THE AUTHOR BALDEV BHATIA

THANK YOU FOR READING MY BOOK

MY SINCERE PRAYERS

FOR ALL MY READERS

"GOD BLESS YOU ALL"

"ANY ONE WHO READS AND KEEPS THIS BOOK AS HOLY MANUSCRIPT, GOD IS SURE TO BLESS HIM, WITH ALL THE PEACE, HAPPINESS, WEALTH, HEALTH AND PROSPERITY OF THIS UNIVERSE"

Baldev Bhatia